Federating Elected Women Representatives of Local Bodies in India

About the Editor

Prof. G.Palanithurai, Rajiv Gandhi Chair for Panchayati Raj Studies, Gandhigram Rural Institute—Deemed University is an academic activist and working with local body leaders, civil society organizations, media, policy community, political parties, donor agencies with a broader objective of strengthening local democratic governance. He has prepared training module, manuals, and administrative manuals for local body leaders and functionaries. He conducts training Programmes for grassroot level leaders. His training is to prepare transformative leaders to transform the rural society. He has to his credit 73 books, 168 articles in referred journals, 95 monographs and 148 popular articles in Tamil dailies in decentralization, governance and rural transformation. He is coordinating the UGC-SAP programme on decentralization. He carried out projects supported by the Ford Foundation, the Hunger Project, the World Bank, the UNDP, UNICEF, DANIDA, Population Foundation of India, Rajiv Gandhi Foundation, Toolkit Foundation of Netherland, State Planning Commission, CAPART, Ministry of Panchayati Raj, Government of India, worth about 50 Million rupees. He held several administrative positions in the university. He was a member in many professional bodies. He served in many committees of the Government of India, and Government of Tamil Nadu pertaining to local governance.

Federating Elected Women Representatives of Local Bodies in India

Edited by
Prof. G. Palanithurai

CONCEPT PUBLISHING COMPANY PVT. LTD.
NEW DELHI-110059

ISBN-13 : 978-93-5125-069-2

First Published 2014

Published and Printed by

Concept
Since 1974

Concept Publishing Company Pvt. Ltd.
A/15-16, Commercial Block, Mohan Garden
New Delhi-110059 (India)
T: 25351460, 25351794, *F*: 091-11-25357109
E: publishing@conceptpub.com, W: www.conceptpub.com
Editorial Office: H-13, Bali Nagar, New Delhi-110 015, India.

Cataloging in Publication Data—*Courtesy:* D.K. Agencies (P) Ltd. <docinfo@dkagencies.com>

Federating elected women representatives of local bodies in India / edited by G. Palanithurai.
p. cm.
Contributed articles.
Includes bibliographical references and index.
ISBN 9789351250692

1. Women—Political activity—India. 2. Representative government and representation--India. 3. Panchayat—India. I. Palanithurai, G. (Ganapathy)

DDC 305.420954 23

To

The Divine Mother

To

The Divine Mother

Preface

One day when I was in my office after interacting with Elected Women Representatives (hereafter I will refer as EWR) in the training programme in the year 1998 two EWRs came to my room. While interacting with them I found that they meet officials, politicians and others in groups and not individually. I specifically asked a question why do you meet the District Collector in group? Are you representing the grievance of the group? For the above two questions they said that they have developed an intuition that group approach will bring rich dividends as they are seeing through Self-Help Groups. Secondly, they are safe. Thirdly, they replied that the Collector has got highest authority vested with powers to manage rural development officials and through him or her direction could be given to rural development officials to cooperate with panchayats to perform the duties and responsibilities professionally. They further informed that though they met the District Collector in group they never addressed common problems but they represented the problems individually they faced in their respective Gram Panchayts. Though they went in group, they had not realized the full potentials of groups. But they got some idea about the group approach. Yet another interesting point I have gathered in the interaction. Somehow or other they are able to achieve something. To create such a feeling they thought that some achievements have to be shown to them without their help and interference. Through their interaction with District Collector they achieved what they wanted to achieve as their grievances small from the perspective of the people and from the viewpoint of the Panchayat leader the issues are big and difficult.

Their mobility has given enormous learning to them. From that day onwards my belief has been changed. I had a belief that through training and building the elected women representatives can be empowered capacitated and through them women in the rural areas can be empowered. But the above event has changed my belief and started thinking that one has to go beyond training to empower women and elected women representatives. I met several such events/incidents which made me to think very firmly that the elected women representatives have to be unionized and they should be in groups. Then we started our journey in federating the elected women representatives. It was initiated by the Ford Foundation with its approach and financial support. We a few partners worked in South India joined together for the new task which was the first initiative of this kind and scale in India.

Tamil Nadu, Karnataka, Andhra Pradesh and Kerala states have been covered in the exercise which was coordinated by Devaki Jain. Later several donor agencies evinced keen interest and supported such a move in India. Of course, the Ford Foundation project brought several successes in Karnataka and Tamil Nadu. Several drawbacks and failures have also been witnessed. Of the four states the experience of Tamil Nadu had been recorded systematically and analyzed and it was published (G.Palanithurai, G.Uma, and J.Vanishree, Networking of Elected Women Representatives at Grassroots, New Delhi: Concept Publishing Company, 2009). After the publication of the book, I have been asked by Devaki Jain to document experiences of all the four states in Federating the elected women representatives and initially I responded positively but I could not do it.

Everywhere, I went I was asked to talk about the experience of the Federation of Elected Women Representatives of Tamil Nadu as I coordinated the activities of the Federation for about seven years. Subsequently, there were many organizations who took responsibility to organize different federations. But there is no organized material for reference and more particularly to serve the researchers. At the university level, Centre for Women Studies has been created with the financial support of the University Grants Commission. Absolutely, there is no connection between the Centre for Women Studies and Elected Women Representatives. In order to take forward this exercise further in a more organized way in the backdrop of the experience we had in organizing the Federation of Elected Women Representatives, SDC, New Delhi organized a workshop in New Delhi. All the participants had shared their experiments of their respective states. Some of the participants had a copy of the book written by me on the experience of Tamil Nadu.

Many participants felt that such a kind of document covering the whole country is needed. Immediately I contacted my publisher Concept Publishing Company's Mr. Ashok Kumar Mittal on this matter. He immediately responded positively. Then I asked my colleagues who participated in the programme to write articles based on their experience in organizing the elected women representatives. Some of them immediately responded positively. But they put a condition that it will not be a research article but a document which gives the process of the journey. Since I agreed, based on their experience some of them have sent their write ups, the publisher asked me to add the report of the workshop also. I contacted Adil Ali. He has agreed to use the document for wider circulation. As a result, a small document is on your hand which gives you the overview of the early experience of the experiments conducted in different states by different agencies for different donors. It provides lot of scope for evolving theoretical aspects of the process of federating the elected women representatives.

G. Palanithurai

Acknowledgements

All the works, coming out from our Rajiv Gandhi Chair for Panchayati Raj Studies, Gandhigram Rural Institute are really the hard work of many people working with me. Like any other work, it is also a work based on the fieldwork. From conceptualization of the concept "Federating Elected Women Leaders" to present many helped. Sometimes help comes from individual. Registering gratitude to them is the need of the hour as good work needs recognition. In this context, I place on record many donor agencies and civil society organizations who have done excellent contribution in this area. Thirdly, the contributions for this book based on their experience they have written article. They are activists. They should be congratulated and appreciated. Fourthly, Preeta Lal and Adil Ali who have taken initiatives to organize workshop and gather the experiences. They deserve our appreciation. Fifthly, the publisher who has accepted my proposal without any hesitation. Because they know that our work is based on our action research. Hence, I have to register my thanks to the Concept Publishing Company, New Delhi. Sixthly, my academic unit in the Department and Rajiv Gandhi Chair deserves my appreciation. My colleagues in the Department and Rajiv Gandhi Chair understood my work pressure and they take routine works in the department and allow me to devote my time for the extension work and research activities. Hence, I have to register my thanks to them. Finally, my family unit extends support in all possible ways to me. My wife Mrs. Mala looks after the house and me also. I register my thanks to her profusely.

G. Palanithurai

List of Contributors

Avani Rawal Network Co-ordinator, Mahila Swaraj Abhiyan, Gujarat.

Bhim Raskar Director (Programme) Resource and Support Centre by Development (RSCD), Maharashtra.

Shyamala C. Vijaya Joint Director, Centre for World Solidarity, Andhra Pradesh.

Uma, G. Assistant Professor, School of Gender and Development Studies, IGNOU, New Delhi.

Vanishree, J. Assistant Professor, School of Gender and Development Studies, IGNOU, New Delhi.

List of Abbreviations

ALGI	Association of Local Governments Institutions
BDO	Block Development Officer
CWS	Centre for World Solidarity
EWRs	Elected Women Representatives
GO	Government Order
GPMSA	Goa Panchayat Mahila Shakti Abhiyan
GR	Government Resolution
JVM	Janpath Vikas Manch
LoGIn	Local Governance Initiative
MRA	Mahila Rajsatta Andolan
NGO	Non-Governmental Organisations
PESA	Panchayat Extension to Scheduled Areas
PEVAC	Pre-Election Voters' Awareness Campaign
PMEYSA	Panchayat Mahila Evam Yuva Shakti Abhiyan
PMM	Panchayat Mahila Manch
PMSA	Panchayat Mahila Shakti Abhiyan
PRIs	Panchayati Raj Institutions
PRSS	Panchayati Raj Sahyog Sangh
RSCD	Resource and Support Centre for Development
SDC	Swiss Agency for Development and Cooperation
SIRD	State Institute of Rural Development
SSF	Singamma Srenivasan Foundation
SSS	Stree Suchana Sangama

UNDP	United Nations Development Programme
VLVM	Vidarbha Lok Vikas Manch
WGWI-G	Working Group for Women Issues in Gujarat

Contents

Introduction

The articles and a report in this book attempt to describe and explain the experience of different stakeholders in federating the elected women representatives of the local bodies in different states of India. The very space created for women at the grassroots institutions legitimately through the 73rd and the 74th Amendments of the Constitution of India for governance and development has created volley of questions and of them one is essentially so important and imperative to answer immediately. The question is, to what extent the elected women representatives are equipped to perform certain hard tasks with less powers and resources in a given patriarchical structure of the society[1]. This question emanated from the basic argument that the local body institutions will deliver goods effectively and efficiently only when the institutions are vested with adequate powers and needed resources. By doing so one can expect collective participation and deliberation at the grassroots on the common issues who have affected the community life. Essential conditions for collective action are giving needed powers and resources for action. Secondly, the needed capacity to manage local institution has to be created and enhanced. Local body institutions are training fround for the representative democracy. The above theoretical argument had been projected by John Stuart Mill. He further enunciated that it is the place where local capacity building will take place for effective functioning of democracy on the whole.

There is yet another argument developed in this context. When seats have been reserved for women in local governance institutions, the role of the representatives has not been changed for women. Both men and women have to discharge the same roles and responsibilities as representatives of the people. But the general expectation is that the Elected Women Representatives (EWRs) have to discharge their role and responsibilities with a different perspective distinctively different from that of men. But the general rule is that women have to occupy the seats more in number to bring change. So their numerical strength matters much. Since, the number of seats reserved for women in local governance institutions is not less than one-third of the total strength of the institutions, one can assume that "critical mass" has been formed. Again there is a theoretical argument that once critical mass is formed, eventually the 'critical mass' will involve in critical development action. The critical mass theory evolved in the West has to be followed in Indian context differently. So carefully the critical mass theory has to be examined in the process of re-examining the critical mass theory one can see easily the impact of socio-economic conditions of the people who constitute critical mass. A new argument is being developed that mere number will not constitute critical mass but the capacity and capability of the members will also count critical mass.

Theoretically speaking, Indian local governance institutions have got more than sufficient number of representatives from the disadvantaged sections and marginalised groups and hence one can assume that critical mass has been formed. Women a distinct category has got some common issues generated biologically. But they are in different socio-economic and political conditions and hence women have to be looked at from the perspective of where they are located. South Asian women and more particularly the Indian women are in different socio-economic settings and hence one cannot presume that simply because they have reached the critical number they can perform the critical functions[2]. A lady can become the President of India, Prime Minister of India, Cabinet Minister, Chief Minister and District Collector, but it is very difficult to become a President of a Gram Panchayat on her own even if a seat is reserved for women. It is further difficult to discharge the responsibilities as representatives in the society on her own. It is also true that there are extraordinarily and exceptionally able and skillful elected women representatives who have excelled elected men representative in terms of performance. Equally yet another set of elected women representatives who are in struggle in their panchayats to transform the rustic folk[3]. The success and struggle of the elected representatives of women have not been shared with other elected women representatives who are unable to even to go nearer to the Panchayat office.

In India one can see the functioning of the Constitution of India and practices of the communities at the grassroots. Wherever, the communities are transforming fastly, community practices have given space for the practice of the provisions of the Constitution and wherever, the communities are in community practices strongly, one could witness the conflict of the community practices and constitutional provisions[4]. There have been open challenges to the constitutional institutions. Throughout India we find traditional institutions in operation. When the traditional institutions have got grip over the community's patriarchy will be in operation[5]. The problems the elected women representatives are facing of different kinds[6] and intensity depending on wherefrom the elected women representatives are drawn. Women have been drawn to local governance space immediately after announcing the seats reserved for women.

Women who contested in the election along with men in the general constituency are always prepared well in advance. In all reserved constituencies for women, they are prepared only after the announcement of the constituencies while Election Commission makes announcement for general election. Most of them are drawn and driven towards to the space by various forces. Hence, they do not have any political orientation even before. Barring a few women, most of them have been drawn to local governance as raw candidates without having any political orientation. Apart from the above elected representatives educational and social background are not uniform. In terms of education they vary from primary education to research degree. And in terms of social conditions most of the elected representatives are from most disadvantaged groups[7]. Yet all the elected women representatives have the same powers to discharge the responsibilities. The elected women representatives who are in the communities which are transforming slowly have to face more number of problems with high intensity than the other places. Hence, the required skill, capacity and capability for elected women representatives are more than the required skill for the men.

But the training offered to women is the same to men in the approved institutions and there is no training perspective and approach apart from teaching them to carry out the activities with the given resources as stipulated by the Central and state governments, in many of the states[8]. The moment the elected women representatives have gone to the community after attending the training programmes in the approved institutions they found totally contradictory to the information provided in the training programme and the reality in the community on governance. The expectations of the people are on the increase from the local bodies, powers and resources available in the panchayats are very limited and the cooperation of the officials is not to the level of expectations and yet they have to deliver. It was narrated by a woman Panchayat president as "my legs are totally tied and I was asked to perform a dance"[9].

The abject conditions of the elected women representatives made one thing clear that they require a different type of training. Further, the elected women representatives need support structure to support them when they are in difficulty. Moreover, they want the official's cooperation and hence they need periodical meeting with officials. To fulfil the above requirements many civil society organisations have started conducting leadership training[10]. New academies have been organised[11]. Different types of training programmes had been carried out. In this context, the elected women representatives have been federated with the support of the Ford Foundation later it was followed by many other agencies[12]. As a result many donor agencies have funded for federation activities of the elected women representatives. Approaches, perspectives, organising methodology vary from organisation to organisation. Most of the elected women representatives' Federations have carried out activities based on the perspectives of the donor agencies rather than on the demand of the Federation. Only a few donor agencies have given free option to the Federation to function on their demand. It is also the reality that within a state many such federations have shrank up and functioned with different perspectives. On a few occasion, we have witnessed conflict among the federations because of difference of perspectives. The federations got visibility; political parties developed a perspective that a major catch of the able elected women representatives can be drawn towards the political party from the federation by bringing the Federations closer to political parties. In the same way, the government has also evolved strategies to respond to the challenges of the elected women representatives' federation. A few federations are always closer to the government and whatever they demanded had been positively responded by the government. A few federations are always opposing the government in order to draw visibility. As a result, they never move with government officials.

Following the experience of the civil society organisation in federating Elected Women Representatives, Government of India has also extended support for such a kind of activities. Government of India has developed framework for evolving federation of elected women representatives. At different levels organisations have carried out activities for strengthening the elected representative's federations. Number of federations has been increased. Visibility has been given to the elected women representatives increasingly. Conflict among the federations appeared in the news papers. The agencies who have facilitated, promoted and organised such federations for elected women representatives were responsible for conflict among the Federations. As a result in some of the regions the federation activities who have come to a halt as the funding agencies have stopped funding projects promoting federations.

In this context, a few logical questions have been raised. Where are the federations of elected women representatives? How are they now? What are the learnings the civil society gained in the process of federating the elected women representatives? How to sustain the federations formed? In order to find out answer to the above questions, a workshop was organised in New Delhi by the Swiss Agency (SDÇ). Almost all the stakeholders have been invited including Government of India, Ministry of Panchayati Raj to solve their experiences. All shared their experiences in the workshop and they are documented. The report of the workshop is also made part of the book. After the workshop my friends asked me to document some of their experiences for wider dissemination. Hence, I have take up this task of compiling all their presentations.

The First Chapter entitled "Mahila Rajsatta Andolan: Campaign for Women in Governance – Maharastra" by Bhim Raskar has explained the whole range of activities, approaches and processes in organising the women leaders in Maharashtra. It is an exciting experience in organising the women for governance in this state.

Second Chapter "Formation and Strengthening of Panchayat Elected Women Representatives in Network in Andhra Pradesh – An Empowerment Strategy" by C.Vijaya Shyamala from Centre for World Solidarity, Hyderabad explained successfully how the Centre for World Solidarity involved in organising the elected women representatives as Federation. The Centre for World Solidarity has taken up the framework of Government of India, Ministry of Panchayati Raj for elected women representatives' Federation of Andhra Pradesh. She explained structure, function, strength and achievements. Here, it is to be noted that Lok Satta in collaboration with the Singamma Sreenivasan Foundation under the leadership of Devaki Jain has organised the elected women representatives from Andhra Pradesh. It was the first experience in Andhra Pradesh. It was done by Lok Sabha.

In the Third Chapter "Panchayat Mahila Manch – Gujaraj: Mahila Swaraj Abhiyan" by Avani Rawal explained the process of federating elected women representatives. In Gujarat they have oriented the Panchayat leaders in perspectives. She heighted not only the approaches but also the impact and experience gained in the process and major achievements made have been covered.

In the Fourth Chapter "Formation of Elected Women Representatives Association in Tamil Nadu" written by G.Uma and J.Vanishree have explained the context in which the federation has been conceptualised. How activities had been carried out and what are the major achievements of that exercise had been explained. The two scholars who have written this chapter involved themselves deeply in this project funded by the Ford Foundation.

Chapter Five entitled "Federating Elected Women Representatives in Tamil Nadu" has been written by G.Palanithurai. In this article he has explained under what circumstances federation activities were thought of and what are the major events of the elected women representatives during that period have been explained. It is almost a work report of the project activities of the Ford Foundation Project in Gandhigram. It is a report of the first phase activities of the Ford Foundation Project in Federating elected women representatives.

Chapter Six is the full-fledged report of the "National Workshop on Strengthening Women Leadership in Local Governments through Collectives and Federations" held from 7th to 9th September, 2010 in New Delhi. It was organised by the SDC. The report gives an idea about the ground realities of Elected Women Representatives Federations in India. The framework under which the whole exercise was carried out has been covered. Based on the past experience where it has to go has been indicated.

NOTES AND REFERENCES

1. There are a number of studies on the performance of the elected women representatives. They are mostly case studies: G.Palanithurai, *Process and Performance of Elected Women and Dalit Representatives*, New Delhi: Concept Publishing Company.
2. Damayanti Sridharan and Rodic Vesna (ed) *Breaking the Political Class Ceiling Women and Local Governance in South Asia*, New Delhi: Fredrich Elbert Stifftung, 2004.
3. The Hunger Project, New Delhi has compiled the stories of Elected Women Representatives published in the Newspapers all-over the country. The successes, struggles and the problems faced by the women leaders have been highlighted in the stories. The *Hunger Project, Thus Spoke the Press*, New Delhi: The Hunger Project, 2008, Vol III.
4. G.Palanithurai and V. Ragupathy, *Communities, Panchayats and Governance at Grassroots*, New Delhi: Concept Publishing Company, 2007.
5. Anirudh Krishna, "Are Villagers Ready for Decentralisation? In L.C. Jain (ed) *Decentralisation and Local Governance*, New Delhi: Orient Longman, 2005.
6. G.Palanithurai, *Empowerment of Women Problems faced by Elected Women Representatives in Local Governance* (monograph) Gandhigram: Rajiv Gandhi Chair Studies, 2001.
7. Government of India, *Study on Elected Women Represenatatives in Panchyati Raj Institutions*, New Delhi: Ministry of Panchayati Raj, 2008.
8. G.Palanithurai, *Dynamics of New Panchayati Raj System: Capacity Building*, New Delhi: Concept Publishing Company, 2009.
9. Tamil Nadu Federation of Women Representatives, *Voices of Women Presidents and Panchayat Governments in Tamil Nadu Chennai*: Human Rights Advocacy and Research Foundation, 2004.

10. The Hunger Project, *Report of the Leadership, Training Programme* Gandhigram: Rajiv Gandhi Chair for Panchyati Raj Studies, 2002.
11. Akash Academy, *Leadership Training*, New Delhi: Akash Academy, 2007.
12. G.Palanithurai, G.Uma and J.Vanishree *Networking of Elected Women Representatives at Grassroots*, New Delhi: Concept Publishing Company, 2009.

1

Mahila Rajsatta Andolan

Campaign for Women in Governance, Maharashtra

BHIM RASKAR

SECTION-I
IN DECISION-MAKING

Mahila Rajsatta Andolan (MRA) has believed in building political consciousness of women and has not restricted itself merely to working with women in politics. MRA asserts that social and political empowerment go hand-in-hand. The problems faced by elected women cannot be viewed in isolation, as women's issues are interlinked and reinforcing. Therefore, there is a need to address women's subordination and its structural causes. The gender discrimination in all sources of power is quite apparent. Men, particularly affluent and upper caste men, hold seats of power and authority. Therefore, MRA believed, women's participation in political decision-making is a crucial step leading to ensure their own rights. This understanding of power, or in particular, unequal distribution of power, meant that MRA seeks to change present political processes in favour of women and weaker sections and to reinstate democratic practices to ensure gender and social justice.

Two slogans popularised in Saigata convention very aptly express the essence of MRA philosophy. The first one was: *'Vote hamara Raj hamara, Leke rahenge Leke rahenge'*, this meant that the vote is ours, the power is ours and we will continue to struggle to get it. This assertion, in particular, averred women's rights as individuals and citizens and declined them as being passive 'vote banks'. The other slogan: *Gavat lokshahi gharat hukumshahi, chalnar nahi, chalnar nahi*; which meant that women want to have democracy within their villages as well as homes, addressed the public-private divide and secondary status women face within their family.

Awareness and articulation of ones' problems often culminates into efforts to tackle those problems. Along this line, this convention too sowed the seed for a state level process, under the banner of Mahila Rajsatta Aandolan. Various sessions discussed need to address issues like water and ration, and implementation of government schemes through Gram Panchayat. Noted social and political activists boosted the morale of struggling women and asserted need for collective and consistent efforts in order to change the situation in women's favour. The Convention discussed the impact and implications of the 73rd Constitutional Amendment and resolved to implement the same in both in letter and spirit in their Village Panchayats. The participants endorsed a charter of demands and took collective oath to plunge into action. In particular, to take active part in decision-making bodies, such as Gram Panchayats and Gram Sabhas, in order to strengthen women's role in local governance and to meaningfully contribute in development processes.

> Objective is to......
> On the 10th of March 2000, more than 1,200 rural women from different villages assembled on the occasion of the death anniversary of Krantijyoti Savitrabai Phule at Saigata village of Chandrapur district. They announced "Mahila Rajsatta Andolan by chanting slogans—*Our Vote.... Our Governance.* These women were either member of their Gram Panchayats, small savings groups or Mahila Mandals. As a result of Mahila Rajsatta Andolan, 145 institutions and organisations are working together in 30 districts, 129 talukas and 841 villages in Maharashtra. Their objective is to encourage women's participation in Gram Sabha and Gram Panchayats.

Source: 'Gender issues' Human Development Report, Maharashtra – 2002.

Saigata convention concluded in an atmosphere of anticipation. It helped to create sense of enthusiasm among the women as well as network partners. Soon after, MRA was launched in over 800 villages covering 30 districts of Maharashtra by total 151 organisations involved in the convention.

'*Saigatanantar kay, Mahila Rajsatta Andolan hai*' (what after Saigata, take Mahila Rajsatta Andolan afar!)—This slogan popularised by women expressed their spirit and agenda post-Saigata. Meanwhile, meetings and discussions involving network partners and women leaders were held to build common understanding about MRA's vision and philosophy. Though it is challenging to thrash out all issues in a collective, it is necessary to build clarity and consensus on some of the important areas of work. The ideological frame of MRA's work, with its vision, mission, objectives and thrust area is given below.

Vision, Mission and Thrust Areas

Vision

A society in which women equally participate in the institution of local self-governance, and are partners in the development processes and thus create an egalitarian, interdependent and human society.

Mission

Strengthening the governance role of elected women members of the Gram Panchayats, other motivated members and development groups by capacity building and creating support system to ensure their active, efficient participation in PRI towards re-building an egalitarian society.

Strategies

The focus will be the groups of women engaged in various regional processes as local Mandals, SHGs, elected women in Gram Panchayats, women political leaders, and building their capacities, perspectives and attitude for enabling them to play effective role in governance.

- Panchayati Raj Institution will be used as important entry point for such women to come into governance role.
- Mass Awareness, social mobilisation and sensitisation.
- A cadre of such women activists will be evolved and trained to take up statewide campaign on identified issues.
- Support system such as cells for information, advocacy, research, training, etc. will be established at taluka, district, regional and state level.
- Convergence of regional issue based processes and efforts of all other actors such as judiciary, media, bureaucrats, NGOs networks among others. For direct linkages with the roles of women in governance.
- RSCD, regional networks and alliance partners will play enabler role in the whole processes and help build inter-linkages of the macro level field situation.

Objectives

- Initiation massive education and awareness campaign on women's equal participation in PRI in identified villages of all districts of Maharashtra and expand future in all-over the state through trained women leaders.
- Evolve capacity building process for identified women leaders, facilitators and also for the development activists at various levels to make them able to reach the goal.
- Create an interdependent support system for village to state in collaboration with existing actors and factors on advocacy, lobbying, research, PRI and women related policies of the state.
- Launch a state level campaign on identified issues and gaps in implementation of PRI, with focus on women's participation for policy change.

MRA Thrust Areas

Perspective Building: Developing a Political Ideology to Strengthen Gram Sabha

Enhancing perspective and attitude of the community members and the network partners, to collectively develop a clear political identity, ideology and perspective for pursuing MRA mission. The focus is on key stakeholders like the PRI members, members from the community (both women and men), social activists, intellectuals, and people from political parties etc., to understand what could be the criteria for strengthening of the Gram Sabha processes.

Capacity Building: Enhancing Potential and Knowledge Building

Capacity building with a focus to enhance self-confidence and assertiveness. This would include—knowledge on PRI functioning, establishing communication with government officials, and developing skills of political negotiation and skill development. Conducting programmes to enhance awareness of women in villages about their rights over village resources and their role in Gram Panchayats and Gram Sabha and also their general political rights. Development of a Support Collective and information dissemination on various policies level issues.

Organisation Building: Developing a Strong Women's Front

Considering the fact that a large number of women who are not actual Gram Panchayat members are part of MRA and have their own agenda of practical needs of gender, violence experienced due to liquor menace, child marriages and severe hunger problems, etc. and which are valid, needs to be addressed as part of the campaign. Hence, framing strong women's front is a priority and a strategy to bring in a large number of women at state level to address issues related to the gender and is a major task. Similarly ensuring at least 50 per cent participation by women in the movement.

SECTION-II
MRA INITIATIVES: PRI FRONT ACTIONS

Any movement evolves and builds on multiple efforts that revolve around its core ideology. Similarly MRA, as a collective effort, has also developed from wide ranging activities carried out from village to state level. These broadly include campaigns, awareness activities, village level programmes, state level processes like advocacy and pressure group, participation in election and governance. This chapter gives an overview of major MRA initiatives and their overall outcome and impact. For the sake of presentation MRA action is divided in three parts: Grassroots Action, Process of Organisation Building and State Level Action, though all are integrally linked.

Understanding ground realities: Post-Saigata period saw a spate of village level activities carried out by the networks with the women. The focus of these activities remained on building awareness on Panchayati Raj with specific emphasis on Gram Sabha and women's participation in decision-making. The sheer number of activities and their reach out reveals the intensity of action post-convention. Total 2274 focus group discussions were organised involving with Self-Help Groups, Mahila Mandals, Anganwadi workers and other key villagers. Total 1800 village level camps were organised for villagers for their awareness building on Panchayati Raj. The total reach out in the first year is about 63,000 men and women.

These wide ranging activities helped to carry forward spirit of the Saigata Convention to the villages. More than anything else these activities helped to realise ground realities and challenges in translating provisions of new PR Act in reality. For instance, though the Act provides for mandatory Gram Sabha meetings, these meetings were either not held, or if held, not in a way they should be. Similarly sub-committees existed only in namesake, even its members being unaware of their membership. Problems of elected women were also innumerable. Lack of knowledge and motivation compelled many to submit to proxy or inactive representation. Wherever, elected women asserted themselves they faced strong reactions from traditional leaders. Thus owing to various reasons, ranging from ignorance to domination, the Act had not got grounding as was desired. Therefore, there was clearly a need to address these problems in a systematic manner.

Self-Help Groups formed ready base: Women's self-help groups have played significant role in inception and growth of MRA. For instance, initially groups already formed by the network partners, became ready launching pad for MRA programmes. In effect, MRA activities did not have exclusive focus on the elected women but were more inclusive in their nature. Various activities involved considerable number of non-elected women and other community members.

Women leaders soon realised importance of self-help groups as their back up structure. A number of women have systematically set up self-help groups and built their constituencies. In a way, MRA offered self-help groups with a very empowering programme to go beyond their group agenda and participate in local decision-making processes.

Campaign to Promote Gram Sabha – Gram Sabha Gaurav Abhiyan

The 73rd Constitutional Amendment recognises Gram Sabha as a dynamic decision-making unit. Gram Sabha is considered as a vehicle to bring about participation of people in making decisions that matter to them. The Act provides detailed guidelines in terms of frequency of the meetings, agenda, procedure to call and conduct them, required quorum and records keeping etc. However, the way this democratic exercise is carried out in reality is quite contrary to the spirit this provision beholds. Problems were innumerable. For instance, people are unable to attend Gram Sabha meetings, simply because proper publicity through prior notices is not given. Practice of adjourned meetings is also common to keep away people from these meetings.

In this context, activating and strengthening this people's forum became the primary concern of MRA. Consequently, campaign to highlight significance of Gram Sabha and to activate these meetings at the village level. This campaign, known as *Gramsabha Gaurav Abhiyan*, was formally launched on 2nd October, 2001 with a thrust on:

- **Empowerment of Gram Sabha** and provision of women's Gram Sabha meetings prior to village Gram Sabha.
- **Decentralisation of power through sub-committees** formed with active involvement of Gram Sabha members.
- **Devolution of finance** to Gram panchayats and utilisation of budget as per Gram Sabha resolutions.

The campaign was launched in a big way using all possible modes of communication and participation. Special slogans were prepared and painted on village walls. A number of pamphlets giving information about Gram Sabha and Committees were distributed throughout the villages. In fact, the Maharashtra government had already published a resolution (GR) on 15th April, 1999, which clearly stated guidelines for Gram Sabha meetings and formation of Sub-committees dealing with education and overall monitoring. The campaign popularised this GR through songs, street plays, rallies and slogans, so much so that the Sarpanch and Gram Sevak could no longer shirk their responsibility. The GR said that the Sarpanch can be removed from the post, if she fails to call Gram Sabha meetings in due time. Though this provision was never actually used, it helped to put across significance of these meetings and corresponding accountability of elected leaders.

The major thrust of the campaign at the village level remained on activating Gram Sabha with people's participation. Similarly, the campaign also urged for policy level changes seeking recognition to Gram Sabha as the supreme body. This meant that all decisions pertaining to village work would be taken in Gram Sabha meetings and these would be considered final. The campaign also demanded that Gram Sabha should have control over all natural resources within the village. The demand for special provision of Mahila Gram Sabha was also put forth. The policy changes were pursued with other like-minded leaders and organisations in the state and in December 2002, the State Government declared the changes enacted to strengthen Gram Sabha. The changes include:

- Allocation of effective powers to the Gram Sabha, as per legal provision enacted in December 2002.
- Women's Gram Sabha now made mandatory before the general Gram Sabha.
- Acceptance by the state government to make appropriate amendments to resolve the issue of adjourned/suspended Gram Sabha.
- Block Development Officers are advised to give adequate publicity to Taluka meetings to ensure participation by women.

The campaign proved successful in reaching out to common people and marginalised sections and resulted in their increased participation in Gram Sabha meetings. More importantly Gram Sabha meetings started to take place. In some villages women demanded that their groups should be informed about these meetings in advance. Women in large numbers started attending these meetings. In some places, members from *dalit* community questioned authenticity of Gram Sabha proceedings on list of BPL families, which was made without really having a meeting. All these changes pointed that a general attitude of indifference is slowly being replaced by a renewed interest and hope in participatory processes of governance. This process of rejuvenation of Gram Sabha, a forum of the people, is a significant achievement of the Gram Sabha Gaurav Abhiyan.

Over the years, MRA has become more persuasive about its primary agenda to strengthen Gram Sabha. After having convinced women to express their views more vocally and people to take part in the village governance, MRA has graduated to take up more strategic issues, such as accountability and transparency, through Gram Sabha campaign. In fact, process of strengthening Gram Sabha has been furthered through various innovative and strategic efforts, including participation in flag hoisting events and demanding Mahila Gram Sahba meetings.

Participation in Flag Hoisting Events

One of the interesting spin offs of the Gram Sabha campaign is MRA's intervention in national day celebrations. Generally women do not take part in public events like Republic or Independence Day. They may take responsibility of cleaning or decorating the venue, but have no role in the programme or the Gram Sabha meetings followed by the programme. Generally Sarpanch receives honour of chairing the function and hoisting the flag on the national days. In villages, where women held this post, the flag hoisting was done either by ex-Sarpanch or some other local leader in the village. Clearly, traditionally powerful local leaders seemed unwilling to share this honour with women and backward class representatives. In a way the true picture of dominance and power got also unfurled with the flag. After experiencing that women Sarpanch in some villages are dissuaded from flag hoisting, women decided to challenge it.

Mahila Rajsatta Andolan (MRA) started a campaign to uphold women's right to participate in public programmes and unfurling flag through the hands of women Sarpanch. This simple step, to be part of national day celebration, caused unrest and led to dramatic incidences in many villages. For instance, in Varve village in Pune district, the women reached Gram Panchayat office sharp at eight to attend the ceremony. They were surprised to see that the flag hoisting was already done. The local leaders were worried that the women would insist for the woman Sarpanch to get a chance. Therefore, they finished off the ceremony before women arrived. In a couple of villages in Marathwada region local leaders openly opposed women and Scheduled Caste Sarpanch who wanted to lead the ceremony. Response of *adivasi* dominated villages in Konkan and North Maharashtra region was quite amicable and community members allowed women to take charge of the programme. While in a few villages in Kolhapur district women were vehemently opposed and criticised for their initiative. Local leaders instigated family members and husbands of these women to stop them from what they thought as 'crossing limits'.

Women enthusiasm was quite evident and they ceremoniously prepared for the national event. In a few villages women rehearsed the national anthem to present on the occasion. Some women's groups decided to distribute sweets to the school children participating in the programme. In Murshidabad village women suggested to make changes in the water supply timings. They suggested starting the supply a little ahead of usual time so that they would finish their work early to take part in the flag hoisting ceremony. Women felt very happy and proud about their participation. By now women's presence in these and such public events has become an accepted norm where MRA is working.

Participation in 'Flag Hoisting event' remained an effective strategy to address both, gender as well as caste discrimination, within the community. MRA's this initiative has been widely appreciated and applauded for its potential to secure women's participation in public ceremonies and soon became an 'official order'. In a national level seminar on 26th September, 2002, chaired by Chief Minister Vilasrao Deshmukh, MRA member Kushavarta Bele presented plight of women and backward caste Sanpanch, especially disregard for their power and position by not allowing them to unfurl flag. The Chief Minister assured to pass an order to stop this injustice and within months a government resolution was circulated, which said that the flag hoisting should take place by Sarpanch and no woman or backward caste Sarpanch would be deprived of this right. This order, which was implemented since 26th January, 2003, has helped large number of women and Scheduled Caste Sarpanch in Maharashtra to have the honour of leading flag hoisting.

Advocating Mahila Sabha

A number of problems encountered in holding of Gram Sabha meetings have been discussed earlier. Many of these arise due to lack of awareness on parts of people and/or lack of accountability of elected representatives and administration. In addition to these women faced a peculiar problem, whenever they went to attend Gram Sabha meetings. These meetings are primarily viewed as men's prerogative, where women's presence is considered unnecessary. If holding Gram Sabha meetings is a challenge, ensuring women's participation in these meetings is an even bigger challenge. Even the women who are quite motivated and informed found it difficult to assert themselves in these meetings. The gender bias was so apparent that when women insisted on attending these meetings, they were humiliated. Women shared that their presence was not taken seriously or sometimes they received derogatory remarks from men. Such experiences were disappointing and gave a sense to women that their initiative is futile. In short, it impacted adversely on women's willingness to attend the meetings. Since, the women's participation did not remain consistent, their concerns could not get reflected in the village planning.

On account of such experiences, MRA decided to advocate for a provision to have special meetings for women, Mahila Gram Sabha, as a way to ensure women's involvement in local decision-making. It was believed that Mahila Gram Sabha will provide women a safe place to get together, in order to understand and contribute to the process of village governance. MRA demanded that Mahila Gram Sabha should take place one day before the Village Gram Sabha meeting. The decisions taken in the former would be duly considered in the later meeting. More importantly, women are expected to attend village Gram Sabha to ensure that their deliberations have a place in the overall decisions. Clearly this was perceived as a stop gap provision, to facilitate confidence and acceptance of women in the village Gram Sabha.

Admitting the relevance of such special meetings, the state government passed a **resolution on 12th October, 2002**, which made it mandatory to organise a 'Mahila Sabha' one day before the Village Gram Sabha. It was also noted that the Sarpanch would be responsible to call this meeting and the Gramsevak would be present to record proceedings.

This Government Resolution was widely publicised in the villages where MRA was working and it led to demand to organise Mahila Sabha. The village women who were in the forefront could mobilise women's participation in these meetings. A study done by MRA, two years after the provision, showed that women are keen to share their problems and express their views on various development matters. Issues such as, toilets, drinking water, rationing, health centre, roads, BPL list etc., have received top priority. Demand for liquor prohibition and employment has also been taken up in some villages. Unfortunately, not many of these concerns were addressed by the local leadership. On the flip side, it was observed that neither local leadership nor the administration is keen to take these meetings. Therefore, despite the state order, Mahila Sabha meetings receive cursory importance and are taken only for namesake. Only where women are aware and are able to put pressure on concerned leaders and authorities, the meetings have taken place somewhat consistently. Interestingly Mahila Gram Sabha meetings have added to distorted perception about women's participation. The Mahila Sabha is considered to be a women's forum and the village Gram Sabha is considered as 'all male' forum.

Despite these lacunae the process of coming together through Mahila Sabha has resulted in improved participation of women in the village meetings. Also, women's unity has been enhanced in the process of their regular meetings and interactions.

Transparency in Utilising Public Funds

Gram Sabha is supposed to be the forum where discussions about the budget are held. Though the decisions of these meetings are not binding on the Gram Panchayat it is potentially an effective forum to facilitate clean decision-making. A vibrant Gram Sabha, among other things, is more likely to ensure identification of genuine cases to take benefit of government schemes, to follow-up collective decisions and to check manipulation of Gram Panchayat funds, if any.

Mahila Rajsatta Andolan (MRA) has taken up several interesting programmes in its endeavour to promote Gram Sabha. In year 2003-04, MRA initiated 'hishob dakhva' (show us accounts) programme. This entailed people should not only participate in Gram Sabha meeting, but should also be aware of the final records submitted by the Sarpanch and Gramsevak on behalf of the village. Thus, people should get to see the copy of actual approved budget and the annual accounts of their Gram Panchayat. People's right to see the records was asserted through this campaign. The provision of 10 per cent budget for women's welfare and 15 per cent budget for underprivileged sections was also ensured through this campaign. This budget was successfully appropriated for the benefit of concerned group of people.

Joint Ownership

Similarly, another remarkable initiative commenced following the Government Resolution (dated 20th November, 2003) to give joint ownership of households. The order urged Gram Panchayats to take decision to include the names of both the husband and wife on the ownership documents of household property. This order gave a tool to assert for women's right on the house they live in and live for. This Government Resolution (GR) was also widely publicised and efforts to push it through Gram Sabha were taken up. In many villages women could successfully lobby for implementation of this GR. Moreover, a public debate could be generated in many more places to justify for the recommendation of GR. Joint ownership could be ensured in a number of villages and new nameplates having names of the husband as well as the wife were displayed. As expressed by many, this change has brought in a sense of dignity and self-assurance among women.

Contesting Elections

Elections are an integral aspect of MRA mission, as being in governance implies seeking power through democratic means. MRA has always encouraged and supported women to be part of elections, as contestants or campaigners. In fact, one of the significant initiatives that followed soon after Saigata convention was spontaneous participation of women in Gram Panchayat elections. Three months after the Saigata Convention (March 2000) Gram Panchayat elections were declared in some parts of Marathwada and Western Maharashtra. Women were quite motivated to contest these elections and be direct part of decision-making bodies. Mostly women decided to contest on seats reserved for them. The motivational levels, both of the women and NGOs supporting them, were so high, that in a few places they even decided to make all-women panels or to contest on open seats. Similar enthusiasm was evident in the Gram Panchayat elections in Konkan that were declared soon after.

Regional networks organised special pre-election training programmes for women who were either aspiring themselves to contest or planning to back women candidate in their villages. Obviously women did not have money or experience to back them. They did not enjoy backing of any political stronghold in the village either. Still they evolved their own strategies for campaigning, which made this effort even more important.

In many respects, this first step in the election fray remained a valuable learning experience. Largely, the efforts remained well meaning but lacked in strategic understanding of the overall process of elections. For instance, there was not much clarity on which panel to choose. And women ended up accepting whichever panel approached them without negotiating with them. Then there were also instances where the panels ignored their women candidates and did not involve them in campaigning at all. Thus, the male members attempted to keep all control with them. Women being inexperienced in negotiation skills succumbed to it. Still in a few exceptional places women expressed their disapproval to such uncalled interference by men and went ahead with independent campaigning with active support from other women. There was also very little awareness about election procedures, particularly about restructuring of wards and process of filing nominations. All the lacunae were addressed to a great extent in the future attempts to participate in the election.

As of now participation in the elections has become an ongoing programme on MRA's agenda. It is difficult to keep count of how many women have contested and won the elections. After having gone through a number of elections, women have now developed better understanding of the election process as a whole. Many women have been elected for two or three times successively. A large number of women have contested for upper tiers of the PRIs, such as Panchayat Samiti and Zilla Parishad. Only recently, Kushavarta Bele from Devani in Latur district, a long time associate of MRA and a dynamic leader, has been elected as ZP member and she heads the Women and Child Development Committee.

Apart from participating in elections, MRA is also active in organising 'Pre-election Campaigns'. These are aimed at building awareness among voters in order to have a free and fair election. Campaign highlights political rights of people, their responsibilities and persuades people to choose a right candidate. Sometimes, campaigns revolve around specific issue or theme. For instance, the focus of recent pre-election campaign in Gram Panchayat election in October 2007 was 'clean elections'.

In spite of such practical experience and orientation elections still remains a challenging period and women encounter various problems. Most often elections turn out to become a power seeking game rather than being a democratic exercise to choose people's representative. Divisive tactics are at its peak in this period. Use of money and liquor is rampant to sway voters to ones' side. Therefore, conflicts with other established contenders are inevitable. Women are pressurised to withdraw their nominations. Sometimes, this pressure is exerted from woman's family members. Thus, election time gives rise to conflicts with outsiders and at times, even with one's own family members. However, the women have developed immense maturity and the way they view their success or failure is fully admirable. There are many women who have not able to win the election. But this has not necessarily deterred them. Some say that it had been a learning experience and some also say that they would try once again.

Undoubtedly elections are fought with an aim to win, but not at the cost of values you believe in. In 2006, Maya Sorte from Vadval village in Latur district contested Gram Panchayat election for the second time. She was contesting election on an open seat against a male candidate, who had three children. Therefore, on the grounds of 'two-child norm policy' adopted by the state government, he was an ineligible candidate. As is a usual practice, he had submitted false personal information to suit the criteria for candidature. A one line complaint from Maya, who was his opponent, would have debarred him from election and given clear line to Maya. Maya's panel members insisted that she should go ahead with the complaint. As a principle, MRA is against two-child norm, which goes against constitutional rights of individual. Therefore, Maya was unwilling to fall back upon this fact to disqualify her opponent. However, her supporters and panel members were not in a position to understand the value based politics she was attempting to pursue. Maya told them that she would make the complaint but in reality, she did not do it. Later, Maya received majority votes and won the seat. More than her victory she was elated by the fact that she has not compromised on her values to succeed. Maya believes that power is just a means and not an end. And many instances in her political life substantiate her conviction.

The practice of unopposed elections is another important issue that women often have to deal with. This can be either very useful or highly imperious exercise depending on the way the consensus is established. If the candidates are really selected by Gram Sabha in a unanimous manner, villagers can be spared of conflicts and costs incurred in election period. Some villages do demonstrate such unity and therefore unopposed elections do not hamper the democratic spirit behind choosing ones' representatives. However, there are also instances where unopposed election is just a facade to disguise control of political strongholds in the village. Particularly decisions pertaining to reserved seats, both for women and Scheduled Caste representatives, are taken on their behalf and these posts are selected rather than elected. Clearly the local leaders choose only those who they think would remain in their control. Interestingly, the state government has a provision of incentive for Gram Panchayat for unopposed election, which means unanimous selection of representatives without taking elections. Since unopposed elections save expenses involved in carrying out election process, part of the amount is given to Gram Panchayat as award. This incentive plan, however, does not delve much into the process of selection to see whether it was really unanimous or domineering.

Over the years women's aspirations have gone up and women

even plan to contest elections for upper tiers, like Panchayat Samiti and Zilla Parishad. Unlike Gram Panchayat elections, these two elections are contested through a political party. Therefore, the aspiring candidates have two options; either they can get a nomination through some political party or they can contest as independent candidates. The later option is workable only if the candidate is strong in his/her work base and resources. The constituencies are much larger and hence campaigning is costly as compared to Gram Panchayat elections. Hence, backing of a political party becomes necessary. Almost everywhere a major challenge before the women wanting to contend at upper tiers is which political party to choose from? It is a challenge before MRA also, which has been vehemently discussed on several occasions.

Various wings of political parties active at village level also attempt to tap women involved in MRA to join in with them. The interests of these political parties in these attempts vary and are situational. Mostly they view MRA members as more active women and feel this group of women as a potential resource to strengthen their agenda.

MRA members are seen capable leaders with strong support system, mass following, and credibility among village people due to their development work. During election period seats are offered to women, especially by political parties having weak mass base, so as to get a readymade women leader for election benefit. Associating with political parties, women are likely to benefit most of the times in terms of wider support, resources, contacts that the respective parties have. There are women who have decided on their own about joining a particular party and still continuing the work of MRA. But there are women who have joined political parties with religious ideologies, which go against the values of MRA, and it has been a challenging experience. These attempts of interference or intervention from political parties also show that MRA members have created a strong position for themselves in the village politics. It indicates recognition to their identity and strength.

At present MRA has framed a broad position, which guides its members to join in an appropriate political party in their area. Clearly, it is beyond a collective's strength to influence national or regional political parties. Therefore, the broad position suggests women that they should join in such political parties who are democratic in their functioning, value secularism and uphold cause of poor and marginalised. These are basic non-negotiable pointers decided upon by MRA while joining in or working within a political party.

In sum, it can be said that MRA views participating in Gram Panchayat elections as a very important strategy to influence local governance. It is an opportunity to reach out to electorate and spread the message one is working for. Therefore, though winning matters, whether one has won or lost the election, does not become the only parameter to measure success. Taking part in election without compromising on ones' value base is considered more important than winning anyhow. It is heartening to see that many MRA women have inculcated this long term vision in them and get into the election fray with an attitude of patience and conviction.

A Landmark in the History

In 2003, the seat of Sarpanch in the Dharne Gram Panchayat was announced as reserved for a Scheduled Caste women candidate. Chayatai expressed her desire to contest the Gram Panchayat elections. However, her opponents started spreading rumours about her, creating a panic among the male that once Chayatai is elected she will sideline them. Therefore, the opponents put forth another women candidate, 'a proxy candidate', who was uneducated and was hearing impaired.

The opponents tried to target Chayatai in every way possible. She had to face double subjugation—one account of being a Woman and two on account of being a Dalit.

Chayatai did not give and decided to fight back, though she was aware of the fact that she lacked the economic power that the opponents boasted. However, she was satisfied that though she did not have money…she had a good work to fall back on.

Chayatai went ahead and filed her nomination papers from both the Scheduled Caste reserved category and the open category seats. Her opponents challenged her move, but the Tehsildar supported her.

However, at the time of announcing the results, the Tehsildar announced the result of the reserved seat alone, in which Chayatai had secured lesser votes. She had actually won in the open category seat. However, the Tehsildar did not disclose those results and directly announced that her opponent had won the elections. When she came to know about this, she opposed the decision and went to fight with the Tehsildar. In the meanwhile, the opponent started celebrating, but the villagers remained confused. The Tehsildar refused to budge and asked her to approach higher authorities. The next 2 days were unfortunately holidays, Saturday and Sunday. On Monday when Chayatai took the Xerox copies of the vote counting documents to the District Level Election Officer, he too turned a cold shoulder. Chayatai warned him that she would go the court and seek justice. On this the Election Officer replied, 'what is the use of going to court? The court will take at least 5 years to give a verdict, by then your term will get over and the entire exercise will be futile!!'

However, Chayatai did not concede. She went ahead and filed a case in the court at Latur. There, when her lawyers saw her papers he assured her that she was right, she had won the elections in reality! This increased Chayatai's confidence manifolds.

However, the court procedures were very lengthy and expensive. Every day a minimum of Rs. 5000 used to be required. Because of the case, Chayatai and her husband were unable to go home during festival time.

Meanwhile in the village, Chayatai's opponents were banking on her absence. They were trying to convince the people that she was wrong and that their candidate was rightfully elected. They also made a new board for the Gram Panchayat, mentioning names of the newly elected members, including their own candidate.

In the court though, justice ruled! The court passed the judgment in Chayatai's favour in a short span of 15 days. She was pronounced as the rightful member of the Gram Panchayat and the membership of her opponent candidate was dismissed. Subsequently, the District Election Officer was suspended.

Chayatai's case was indeed a landmark in the judicial history. It is, therefore, rightly used as a referral case in the Maharashtra State Act.

Participation in Governance Process

Women are still considered to be backdoor entrants, selected at the mercy of reservations and, therefore, acceptance as representatives does not come easily their way. At the same time, there is also an overbearing sense of anticipation towards them and women are expected to prove themselves. Most of the times women's work as representatives begins within a hostile environment. Clearly challenges before elected women representatives, especially who take their work seriously, are many. The representatives belonging to *dalit* or other underprivileged sections also face severe resistance from upper castes when they attempt to exercise their political power. It is a fact that women have to operate within a social context that is patriarchal, divided by class, casteist, communal and as a result constricting. Therefore, what is possible is determined to a large extent by this social context. However, these critical impediments arising of social structures are not the only constricting issues. The structure itself, within which the representatives have to work, stands on a shaky ground.

Though the 73rd Constitutional Amendment grants autonomous status to Gram Panchayats, these bodies are still viewed as implementing agencies by the administrative machinery. Even within the village, the power centre lies somewhere outside purview of democratically elected bodies and caste panchayats or Gavki remain dominant structures influencing local decision-making processes. The devolution of funds as directed by the Amendment is yet to take place and therefore Gram Panchayats are not financially strong and independent. This wider context sets the stage for understanding any interventions, including MRA, that attempt to strengthen grassroots governance processes.

Opposition to Proxy Members

The very first task that the MRA supported elected women took upon themselves was to assert for women's representation within the Gram Panchayat. It is not quite uncommon that husbands or other male relatives of the elected women work on their behalf. These proxy members even attend meetings saying that the concerned women members either do not have time from household work or do not understand the Gram Panchayat work. These excuses are easily acceptable in a patriarchal set up and proxy members continue to enjoy authority and status that in reality is meant for their women counterparts.

In many villages MRA backed women members opposed such proxy representation. When the very first Gram Panchayat meeting of the newly elected body took place, women members urged for real members to be present. Male members thought otherwise. 'Why the women be bothered, let them just come to give signature and go back. This is how it was so far.' But the active women members insisted that elected women representatives should only participate and even if they do not know anything they will learn over the time.

Mahila Rajsatta Andolan (MRA) members are equally aware of their own responsibilities and participate in every Gram Panchayat and Gram Sabha meetings. They also mobilise women for Gram Sabha meetings. The women also have played active role in formation of development committees and making them active.

Capacity Building

In order to make women's participation in decision-making bodies more active and effective they need to be well versed with the procedures of functioning. Here comes the role of capacity building and training to make elected women more knowledgeable and articulate. MRA has engaged in such training programmes since beginning. The process of training and capacity building has also evolved over the years.

Largely capacity building is aimed at enhancing self-confidence and assertiveness of elected women by imparting important information, inculcating perspective of value based politics and enhancing skills for better functioning and negotiation. These training programmes cover practical information on PR and government schemes and information on various Government Resolutions (GRs) that are important for Gram Panchayat functioning. The programmes also give exposure to Panchayat and Zilla Parishad offices and hold interactions with government authorities, gramsevak. Programmes also have specific sessions to upgrade skills, such as budget preparation, etc. The training programmes are participatory and interactive and encourage personal sharing by women to facilitate mutual learning process.

The need of systematic inputs to elected women was recognised by MRA since beginning. The capacity building programmes enhance knowledge and confidence of elected women in their work. In the initial years training programmes were organised at taluka levels. In later years, in association with The Hunger Project, the programmes were carried out for a cluster of villages and the women participants were also encouraged to form a forum at taluka and district levels.

Mahila Rajsatta Andolan (MRA) believes that process of capacity building cannot be restricted to class room teaching. The process of capacity building can be initiated with training programmes, however, several other activities are required to develop and sustain the change process. Therefore, experiential learning of the women through their participation in local level governance process, issue based campaigns and community mobilisation is considered equally important. MRA has also evolved innovative exercises to develop understanding of elected women and local women leaders about the challenges in the governance processes. One such exercise is 'Vastav Darshan', which means understanding reality by studying status of Gram Panchayat functioning. The women are expected to visit five Gram Panchayat in their vicinity and take all possible information about its functioning by talking to elected women. The villages not associated with MRA were selected for this exercise. Similarly, Gram Panchayat Darshan or visits are organised for women to overcome shyness of visiting the office and interacting with the representatives and gramsevak. Gram Panchayat Darshan has helped in making the local governance processes more familiar and information more accessible. In order to provide need based inputs and information to elected women MRA is also planning to develop regional level centres within the state.

Towards New Paths

Archana Jatkar was elected as the Sarpanch of the Pokhari Gram Panchayat in September 2006. When she assumed office as the Sarpanch, the situation of the Pokhari Gram Panchayat was very gloomy!! Gram Sabhas were never held in the village, traditional power holders and local leaders had an upper hand in the haphazard decision-making of the village, women were apprehensive about participating in the public meetings. Given this reality, the first task at her hand was to activate the Gram Sabhas and elicit women's participation in the developmental work of the village.

She called for a women's meeting at her own house. However, she received a very poor response for this attempt, with only 10 -12 women showing up. Nevertheless, Archanatai did not give up. She initiated a dialogue with the women, urged them to come forward and contribute for the development of their own village, ignited a sense of ownership in them. Her efforts were duly paid off when the number of women attending the next meeting surged to 70. It was at this meeting that Archanatai put forth the idea of forming women Self-Help Groups (SHGs). The idea was so appealing and participation of women so active that within 3 days eight women SHGs with a membership of 15 each were formed.

The village had a severe water crisis. However, in spite of repeated requests, the men folk of the village turned a deaf ear. When she appealed to the people to help her implement the Water Supply Scheme in the village, some men opposed. She called a meeting of the SHGs and suggested that they should contribute for the building of a well in the village. Her suggestion was readily accepted and each SHG contributed Rs. 2000. Apart from this, Archanatai appealed for contributions from other people in the village. Even in this endeavour, women were at the forefront. Women, working as daily labourers and earning a meager sum of Rs. 25 to 30 per day, came forward and contributed whatever amount they could afford. As a result, a good amount was collected to dig the well.

A place near the river was chosen to dig the well. The initial 1st instalment under the Water Supply Scheme reached in time and with the help of the money collected by the villagers the first phase of digging the well went off smoothly. However, the second instalment under the scheme was delayed and the work of the well was stalled. However, the Village Cleanliness and Water Supply Committees came forward to support and assured that they will work day and night to see that the work of the well is not stalled. Nevertheless, money was a problem. Therefore, Archanatai decided to shell out money from her own pocket! Within a month, the well was ready and the village was relieved of the long drawn water crisis. The second instalment came only 2 months later!

While ensuring the development of the entire village, Archanatai consciously worked for the deprived sections of the village. The Dalit settlement in the village often experienced waterlogging. Therefore, the work of widening the gutters was undertaken.

Archanatai also discovered that the Panchayat body prior to her had encouraged corruption, taken Rs. 5000 from a widow and promised her a house under the Indira Awas Yojana (IAY). However, after they lost the elections, they backed out and she was duped off her money. This widow came to Archanatai for help. Archanatai took her to the Panchayat Samiti office. The ex-Gram Sevak and Ex-Sarpanch, who had mislead the widow earlier warned Archnatai saying that 'good women do not go to Panchayat Samiti office'! However, Archanatai did not relent and stopped only when the widow received her dues.

Another achievement in her work has been that crop loans have been made available for farmers at a low interest of 1 per cent. Their district being a part of the Vidarbha region, witnessing the highest number of farmer suicides, these loans have proven to be of real help to the burdened farmers. In 2010, Archanatai was again elected with major votes. Her panel will get core leadership in new Panchayat

No Confidence Motion

Men leaders either try to co-opt newly elected women or if that does not work, pressurise them to step down. The provision of no confidence motion is often used against women who the established leadership finds troublesome. Several women Sarpanch face 'no-confidence' under pretext of their lack of capability to work. The real reasons often lie in the local power dynamics and the role women are expected to play within these schemes of things. In the present scenario, provision of no-confidence is largely misused against women who are assertive and do not succumb to pressure.

MRA confronted issue of no-confidence, for the first time, in case of Sumitra Kanhant. Sumitra, a young, unmarried, active and cheerful leader from Warli adivasi community and a resident of Satkor village in Thane district contested election in May 2001. Earlier she had worked to close down liquor shops in the village and was actively involved in several other women's activities. Sumitra received highest number of votes and was even selected as Deputy Sarpanch. The Sarpanch, Damu, was also a young boy, having no past experience about political work, but eager to make most for his village. This Gram Panchayat body implemented several government schemes in one year. The earlier Sarpanch was very upset for losing power and started working against the newly elected Damu and Sumitra with the help of their opponents in the body. Some of members were upset with Sumitra for her opposition to liquor sale in the village. Within months the ex-sarpanch succeeded in taking majority members to his side and made them pass a no-confidence motion against both. Local liquor peddlers supported the opponents. Sumitra had never thought her opponents would go to this extent and put false allegations on her. She was hurt as they had called her incompetent. The appeal against this motion could not be made within stipulated time and Sumitra lost her post. MRA raised this issue at state level appealing various forums, such State Women's Commission and the state government, to take appropriate action. A fact finding team was immediately sent to the village to bring the real picture to the fore. Though the overall atmosphere in the village was tense, a number of villagers were in support of Sumitra and Damu. Over a period Sumitra came out of shock and again started actively participating in Gram Panchayat functioning as a member.

At MRA level, Sumitra's case became a rallying point to highlight misuse of no-confidence to debar active members and to protect interests of local strongholds. Other similar cases were also publicised through media and were presented before the state government. All these efforts led to a policy change in favour of women representatives. A no-confidence motion against Sarpanch or Deputy Sarpanch is passed when two-third members in Gram Panchayat body vote in favour of it. The margin of vote was increased from two-third to three-fourth in case of women representatives.

This change in policy indicates that the government has taken note of the problem and is willing to provide protection to elected women representatives. The policy change was expected to have put some check on rampant misuse of the provision. However, reality shows that elected women still confront no-confidence, especially when they attempt to question local leadership. Recently, Lata Chikram, a woman Sarpanch in Chandrapur Vidarbha region faced no-confidence motion. For two years the majority in the body had no problem with her. In fact, they appreciated her initiative in carrying out sanitation drive in the village with women. The village received an award and someone else was sent to get it on behalf of the village. Lata felt insulted and asked the members why they sent a member to receive an award instead of Sarpanch, who had worked for it? The members disapproved her courage to stand for herself and passed a no-confidence motion against her.

Protection Along with Reservations

The women members who are active or who confront local power holders are also met with mental and physical harassment. When women realise their rights and get empowered to assert them a reaction is bound to occur. A number of such cases have been so far dealt by MRA members. MRA has also proactively intervened when such instances took place outside their own area of work.

When Sunita Aghar from Shirasgoan in Yeotmal district became Sarpanch the local leaders became very upset. For last twenty years the post was held by a single man. Since the post of Sarpanch was reserved he had to give up his control. Sunita got a chance to become Sarpanch, but did not get support from the members. The ex-Sarpanch interfered in functioning and always dominated meetings. Once in a Gram Sabha meeting he got so agitated that he threw chili powder on Sunita's face. The meeting was disrupted and people dispersed. Sunita immediately went to police station to lodge complaint against the villagers who attempted to harm her. The police refused to take the complaint. Local MRA activists soon got the news and rushed to the spot. They accompanied Sunita to police station and then the complaint was properly lodged.

When the woman belongs to a socially backward community, the resistance gets more severe. Nanda Nikam from Bhodni village, in Indapur Block in Pune district, belongs to *Chamar* caste and was selected as Sarpanch, as the post was reserved for OBC woman. The upper caste members did not co-operate with her. They even harassed her in ways hoping Nanda would get frustrated and resign on her own. However, Nanda decided to fight back and went to lodge a complaint against physical assault on her. The police neither filed FIR nor gave her protection she asked for. Here too, MRA activists visited the aggrieved woman and supported her to lodge complaint and get protection.

Such instances are abundant and lots of them even do not become known for a long period. The prevalent gender and caste biases work against elected women who attempt to exercise their political power. Such instances also indicate that provision of reservations would become effective when women are assured of support and protection. Otherwise women would not be willing to go against their family or community to take on challenges that their new role demands. Owing to reality MRA thinks providing Protection to Reservations is must. In this context, MRA has demanded setting up of grievance redressal centres at district level. This demand was raised and unanimously approved in a national level seminar organised by the Maharashtra State Women's Commission with MRA (organised in Mumbai on 26th and 27th September, 2002). It was expected that these centres would provide timely support and guidance to elected women who face harassment or pressure of any sorts, including unjustified no-confidence motions. Such a mechanism would certainly help women struggling at their own level. However, it has still remained very much at the conceptual level. Clearly concerted and collective efforts are required to create the necessary political will in ensuring any protective mechanisms or measures for elected women.

Percentage Raj

On 28th December, 2002, Ms.Vimal Shirsath elected as Sarpanch in the first time of Babulgaon's history, one woman that too, from *dalit* community became the Sarpanch. It was not surprising that because of this; male ego got hurt. In the beginning she was under tremendous pressure because of heap of applications and complaints. She wondered why so much applications are pending? What are the real issues of people? She started studying all this and started her work with the aim of village development. She observed that, in last 50 years, Gram Sabha had took place only on papers not in reality. People were unaware of what is Gram Sabha? When it should be called?

Ms. Shirsath started conducting Gram Sabha. To aware people about the Gram Sabha she used the medium of "Davandi" (public call). She believes that Gram Panchayat is the platform for both villagers and Gram Panchayat body to raise problems as well as discuss remedies and development work. Along with Gram Panchayat Secretary, she started giving information to the people about the Government schemes. People found it very helpful. So people were admiring her. They started respecting and supporting Ms. Shirsath in her every work. She also sees that people's participation should be on a large scale in village governance. Politician in the village didn't like this. It was difficult for them to digest that a woman from *dalit* community is going ahead.

From here the 'Percentage Raj' had started. They joined their hands with opposition members in Gram Panchayat. They started demanding commission in each work of Gram Panchayat. Ms. Shirsath opposed this very strongly. As a result oppositions brought 'no confidence motion' against her. But her good work saved her from all this trouble. Ms. Shirsath implemented various schemes for village development. The main problem of the village was water shortage. She solved this problem by installing hand pumps in village. She sanctioned separate water line for *dalit* colony. Streetlights in village, construction of public toilets, construction of drainage system in the village and issuance of land for construction of houses of landless villagers, are some of the works done by Ms. Shirsath.

Demoralising Tactics

Character assassination is repeatedly used to demoralise women who challenge existing stereotypes and assert themselves. Women leaders involved in MRA have faced such intimidations on several occasions. Working as a Sarpanch demands interacting with villagers, co-members and government officers, who happen to be mostly men. When women relate to men, even as part of their work, they invite criticism. Ratnamala Vaidya is working as a Gram Panchayat member for three consecutive terms since 1994. She has even contested election for Zilla Parishad. Her popularity and work base made her a strong contender and opponents used all possible tactics, including character assassination to demoralise her. She was portrayed as a woman with 'loose character'. The opponents went to an extent to disseminate hand-outs, which painted her as a 'bad woman'. MRA supported Ratnamla to stand firm and respond to baseless allegations. Women who do not get any support in such trying circumstances often succumb to pressures, get demoralised and withdraw themselves in the end.

Woman from backward communities have a tougher time, as they have to fight against caste prejudices as well. There is a strong opposition to their becoming Sarpanchs. Jyoti Meshram from Kotgal Gram Panchayat in Gadchiroli district is perhaps a representative example of how upper caste men resist sharing of power with women from a *dalit* community. In 2002, Jyoti was elected as Sarpanch for this eleven-members Gram Panchayat, as the post was reserved for a Scheduled Caste woman. Jyoti is an educated woman and enjoys very good support from her family and community. She was quite motivated to take up the responsibility. However, upper caste leaders did not approve of her authority, especially her control over Gram Panchayat funds. In the very first Gram Sabha the upper caste lobby pressurised the meeting to pass a resolution which said that the Sarpanch would not have any authority over financial transactions. The responsibility was handed over to another member belonging to upper caste and Jyoti remained deprived of any rights associated with her post.

Support Mechanisms

Women need a supportive and enabling environment that would help them deal with any kind of resistance. Where women have a local support base, either women's groups or their own community members, they are able to fight back. The voluntary organisations can also play an important role in providing support at crucial times. When the elected women are able to fall back on any of such support structures, they are able to work more strongly and effectively. Similarly, being part of group or network broadens perspective of women members and enhances their self-confidence. Many women who have been associated with MRA have changed and developed over the time. Realisation of being part of a strong and successful collective itself inculcates positive attitude and sense of solidarity among women.

Building such collectives is not only important as support structures to elected women but also to make them accountable. The sense of accountability is fundamentally important to engage in value based politics. Women's participation implies that they represent concerns of women and underprivileged sections and make use of their authority to address their concerns. Therefore, what kind of politics women are engaged in also matters when we support and promote their participation in decision-making. It is likely that elected women follow established models of politics and think in terms of individualistic and short-term gains. Such participation is clearly not going to be interest of majority of women. What is power for?, is an important question that the women representatives have to answer and this accountability can be sought by the women's groups and other community based groups that support them. Thus, building local groups and organisations proves to be a mutually beneficial phenomenon for elected women as well as village women at large.

Vijaya Bahirat from Kurkundi village in Sangamner Block is a Sarpanch as well as active member of self-help-group. She was a Gram Panchayat member in the previous body and was not very aware about her role that time. Occasionally she attended meetings, that too only to give her signature. However, in her consecutive term, being associated with MRA, she became more aware. With active support from self-help-groups in her village she has been able to regularise Gram Sabha meetings. The women collectively planned to do *shramdan* for constructing approach road to their village. Later, Vijaya managed to get a proposal for road construction passed by the Gramsevak.

Archana Jamkar from Pokhari village in Pusad taluka in Yeotmal district openly admits that women in her village are her source of strength. Archana formed three self-help-groups soon after she got elected in September 2005. Thus, she developed close connection with a group of 45-50 women. She motivated the women to take part in Gram Sabha meetings. Archana observes that when women are present in Gram Sabha meetings, she feels more confident to address the meeting. The women also backed her in the developmental programmes that she planned. The Gram Panchayat was to raise Rs. 15,000 from villagers to get a drinking water scheme for the village. General public appeals to give contributions did not required amount. The time was running out and hence Archana discussed the problem with the group members. The three groups together gave Rs. 15,000 to Gram Panchayat and later also made home visits with the Sarpanch for recovery. The women also accompany Archana whenever she has to visit Panchayat Samiti or Zilla Parishad offices. Thus, Archana and a number of women like her have been able to create their own support base through self-help-groups.

Many such examples can be cited to show how elected women associated with MRA have mobilised women, in some villages' mobilised communities, as their support group.

Sensitising Men

Another strategy used to counter local resistance is to associate male sympathisers with MRA process. Support from men is hard to achieve unless they are convinced that women are equal members of society and have been disadvantaged historically. Reservation to women is just one of the mechanisms to address this injustice being done to women so far. MRA has carried out Jotiba Jagruti Abhiyan, which is a way to create men's support group to women's initiatives. Abhiyan is aimed at identifying and creating opportunity for men to support and help women leaders.

Similarly, support from the family is very crucial for the elected women to continue in politics and to effectively carry out their roles. Apart from sensitising men on this issue, MRA also promotes positive role models. A family appreciation letter 'Kutumb Sanman Patra' is presented to families who respect and support women's activism. This certificate has helped in increasing the support from family members to EWRs.

In order to enhance confidence of newly elected women and earn them community acceptance MRA also organises a public programme to felicitate newly elected members. These often form an important step towards building an enabling environment for women representatives.

The grassroots action has thus evolved and widened at several levels. As a result of these consistent local level attempts, MRA is now being viewed as forum for justice and equality. On the positive side, involvement of village women in local decision-making processes has increased considerably. Women approach EWRs with several issues, which are governance related as well as other. Therefore, Elected Women Representatives (EWRs) are taking up different women related cases on issues of violence, dowry, rape, or atrocities on Dalit women or even general issues like Public Distribution System (PDS), water, and health and so on. All this has helped in making the local Government institutions more functional and accountable to people and their issues.

Find a Challenge and You Will Find Belebai!

Kushavarta Bele from Devani village in Latur district is a committed and confident leader. Inspired by participating in Saigata convention she first became an active member of Gram Panchayat. Within a span of eight years she has emerged as a political leader and is currently holding the post of Sabhapati of Women and Child Development Committee in Latur Zilla Parishad.

A hard core social activist at heart Kushavartatai has never followed conventional ways to rise up the political ladder. Rather she has always reflected on political tactics of her co-members and remained critical about manipulative ways to get political mileage. She shares, 'Village politics and village matters have 60 per cent truth and 40 per cent dishonesty in them. As a social worker, I am upset by this. Dishonesty is not justified. However, one cannot force honesty all the time. However, I have very strongly demanded that when poor, landless and the needy come for help, they must not be troubled for money. No money should change hands for certifications. I don't tolerate this at all.'

Kushavartatai has made efforts to put more life in the Gram Sabha of the village, making women's participation in them more visible and vocal. Narrating an incident in one of the Gram Sabhas she says, 'The issue was regarding distribution of land for housing purpose. Women were also present at this Gram Sabha. Just as the Sabha was to begin, it started pouring. The crowd began dispersing. It looked like there would be no Gram Sabha. The register was kept at one end and people were asked to sign it. As it was an important issue, I expressed that the Sabha must be held. People waited and a list of 45 people was approved in the Sabha. We saw to it that the real needy were included in the list. I then proposed that the plots distributed should be in the name of the woman. With discussion, it was agreed that the plot should be in the name of both – the husband and the wife. However, how would all agree to this? Some tongues waggled – you say that put your wife's name too and what if she ran away tomorrow? Many nodded their approval. Then we had to raise the question as what would a wife do if her husband ran away? After that, our proposal was accepted.'

Fighting a close battle, she won the Zilla Parishad election and became head of Women and Child Development Committee. In the very first meeting she raised a simple question as to why were men served chilled water in bottles whereas women served normal water in glasses. This was just an example as too how deep-rooted were the simple discriminating norms in the society. All women, with the support of a few men, stopped this practice. She politely challenged the clause stating that said that budget allocations for women should be a minimum of 10 per cent. She raised the point that minimum 10 per cent did not mean only 10. Speaking for the women, she got a raise of Rs 5 lakh in the budget. This is just the beginning. Belebai does not fight for herself. She, who would walk for miles from one village to another, has been given an ambassador car. It is filled with activists and women. She feels that a jeep would have accommodated more activists.

State Level Actions

Apart from the village and taluka level activities, MRA also organised state level programmes, such as conventions and seminars, for women to come together and share their experiences. State level programmes have been organised with an aim to consolidate the grassroots processes and plan future strategies of the collective. State level programmes, especially MRA conventions, have also helped in broadening the scope of MRA work and build strategic linkages to ascertain wider impact. Thus, field level action is very well supported by active state level processes. These various state level activities include:

- *MRA State Conventions*, which have helped in consolidation of grassroots processes and transfer of ownership and leadership.
- *Dissemination of relevant information* from time to time to strengthen grassroots action. Several publications have been produced for proper and timely dissemination of information. Similarly, publications are also produced to share MRA work and achievements and generate wider level debate and support.
- *Policy advocacy* has remained one of the strongest areas of work at the state level. Similarly, media advocacy also has been done effectively. State level action also includes Lobbying with political parties on specific issues and alliance building. The process of state level initiatives, including MRA Conventions shows how the movement has graduated and consolidated its action in a forceful manner.

- *Saigata convention* in March 2000, presented charter of women's demands, initiated collective process of MRA and motivated women's participation in Gram Sabha meetings and Gram Panchayat elections.
- In *Sangamner Convention* in June 2001, Self-Help Group members played a key role in organising the event. Women's initiative in the convention was noteworthy. The convention decided to take up Gram Sabha awareness campaign. And also decided to initiate MRA *Gav shakha*, village unit as a support mechanism for elected women.
- In *Aurangabad Convention*, in June 2002, MRA explored possible linkages and alliance building of women in governance with other critical issues, such as livelihood issues, violence against women and fundamentalism.
- At the *World Social Forum*, in Mumbai in January 2004, over 100 women leaders from across the state actively participated to share their experiences and concerns on a global forum.
- An *International Dialogue* meet took place in Pune in June 2005, with the delegates associated with the Hunger Project from USA and Bangladesh. This meet was helpful in bringing forward challenges faced by elected women. A collective reflection process took place to take stock of strategies, structures and alliances made by MRA to meet these challenges.
- *Strategy building* to develop PRI women's front finalised in Nagpur 2006.
- The latest state convention in *Gargoti* (district Kolhapur), in March 2007, initiated the handing over process to women's front.

MRA Structure

Today MRA is working in 26 districts, 78 blocks, 4 regional networks, with 175 organisations, 40 grassroot women leaders. The regional networks include, (a) Vidarbha Lok Vikas Manch (VLVM) for Nagpur and Amrawati region, (b) Marathwada Lok Vikas Manch (MLVM) for Marathwada region, (c) Janpath Vikas Manch (JVM) for Western Maharashtra region, and (d) Some parts of Konkan region. Almost

1800 EWRs are directly associated in MRA process, as members of MRA Gram Shabha and PRI women's front.

The present structure of MRA, responsible to coordinate state and grassroots action has evolved through a process of democratic dialogue. One of the striking finding of review carried out in 2005 was lack of adequate representation of women members in the state level decision-making processes. The review team commented that though MRA seeks to become a women-led process, it still has very much remained NGO-led process. As women's leadership grows stronger, grassroots women should become legitimate part in the overall decision-making process. MRA team organised a strategy planning meeting in Nagpur in 2006 and plan its future course of action in the light of review findings. The meeting decided to make a drastic change in the structure in order to involve emerging women leaders in the state level decision-making. At present MRA has developed a village to state level structure and has also formed a state level executive committee, giving priority to women's representation. Fig. 1.1 shows the present structure and composition of state execution committee, which is functional since December 2006.

Alliance Building

Reaching out and forming alliances with other like minded groups has remained one of the integral strategies in order to initiate and build effective advocacy processes on several issues of concerns. Since active alliances provide a broader collection of skills and enrich capacities to address issues at hand, MRA has believed in formation of alliances, though formal structures, unless it is necessary, have been avoided. MRA views alliance building as a disciplined effort to create a chain of change agents which can shape and guide various campaigns and actions. Alliance building process has taken place at state as well regional and district levels.

Planned Alliances have been formed with organisations who are closely associated with issues of grassroots governance and are involved in the regional level action plans as well. These include NGOs like Dr. P.V. Mandlik Trust, Sampark, Rationing Kriti Samittee and government/semi-government programmes like MRCP and MAVIM. Supportive Alliances have been formed with organisations and

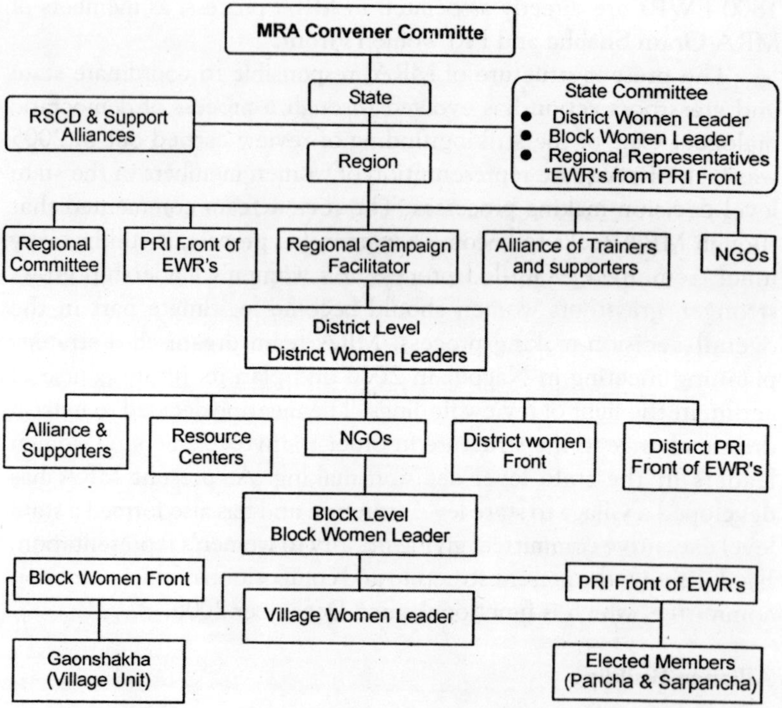

Fig. 1.1: MRA structure.

networks who are playing crucial role to extend support and solidarity from time to time and contributed with their specific areas of expertise. These include NGOs like Aalochana, Yashda, Indian Centre for Human Rights and Laws, AVEHI, NCAS and so on. MRA is also in a process of identifying Potential Alliances for effective work and these include networks and organisations who are taking up broader issues of gender and caste discrimination and sustainable livelihood. These include Anganwadi Worker's Union, AFARM and so on. Apart from these state level alliance partners regional level MRA units are also part of collective struggles specific to their region.

SECTION-III
ORGANISATION BUILDING PROCESS

MRA's inception lies in the initiative taken by network of NGOs. Though it initially started as a project to empower EWRs and strengthen their Governance Roles in Panchayati Raj, it was conceived as a collective process and a movement with grassroots women as its main stakeholders. Thus, MRA has gradually shifted from a project mode to a process mode keeping women and their leadership at the core. With experience and newer insights the work process has systematically led to building of an organisation of women. The organisation building was viewed essential to transfer ownership to women and also to sustain change processes MRA has taken up.

The need for organisation building of women was deemed necessary so as to overcome limitations of NGOs in taking part in local politics. NGOs being outside agencies have limited role to play in village level governance processes. Though they can facilitate and support local women, they themselves are not able to play any active part. Thus, need to empower women themselves become imperative. Very often women get strength from a collective identity, which works as a pressure group. Thus, as more and more women and women's groups became active at the local level, it created necessary ground for required role reversal. Consequently, women's groups took lead role and NGOs and network took a back seat to provide support as and when required.

In the state level convention in Sangamner in 2001, this felt need to initiate organisation building process was voiced for the first time. The convention also passed a resolution and decided to form village level units of MRA. Soon after the convention active women's groups started setting up these village units or *gav shakha*. Though it took 2-3 years to form and activate MRA *gav shakha* in all the work area. Village level units were viewed as a forum of all women as against the SHGs, which can encompass only its members and has a specific agenda. MRA unit became a forum to take up critical issues of governance and other pressure group to address women's concerns. Each unit has a head and an executive body who take responsibility to keep unit active and vibrant. The existence of *gav shakha* is made known to public by setting up a board, preferably at the entrance of the village, just like the political groups usually do. *Gav shakha* collects a nominal membership fee from its members, which is used for local level activities. These units have played important role in election period by supporting women candidates and also in strengthening Gram Sabha meetings. Recently even a programme code is decided to maintain uniformity of procedure in conducting activities and build collective spirit among different units. For instance, the local programmes begin and end with a particular song highlighting MRA vision and demands, sloganeering and oath taking is done to reassure commitment. Women members proudly wear MRA badges and identity cards and paying respect to social champions Jotiba Phule, Savitribai and Babasaheb Ambedkar is integral part of the programme. Overall formation of these *gav shakha* can be considered as a beginning of the MRA, as an organisation.

Over the period, large number of women who are not elected representatives got actively associated with the MRA process. *Gav shakhas* became a collective unit to address all gender and caste concerns of its members. For instance women had their own agenda of practical needs of gender, domestic violence, child marriage, etc. which could be discussed and addressed on these village forums. All these village units combined to become a strong state level front of women active on micro as well as macro level issues of gender and caste discrimination. The state women's front or MRA organisation has primarily focused their energies at three levels:

(i) Increasing membership and strengthening organisation,
(ii) Building awareness among women to empower them by realising their potential and minimise their dependency, and
(iii) Asserting for a political space and political identity.

At present total 285 MRA *gav shakhas* have been formed with total membership exceeding 12,000 women.

Panchayati Raj Women's Front

In the meantime, MRA realised that elected women representatives have specific set of needs, apart from gender, caste specific needs that they share with other women. Field experience indicated several critical problems faced by EWRs, ranging from illiteracy to harassment by local power holders, which needed to be addressed systematically. Here also MRA felt the need to build confidence of EWRs through information and knowledge sharing and skill enhancement and also to create a support group of EWRs among themselves. This idea was brainstormed for a time and in 2006 in a meeting in Nagpur MRA decided to form a separate front of elected women to exclusively focus their issues. Thus, Panchayati Raj Women's Front has been formed at the level of each taluka to facilitate organisation building of EWRs, to enhance their confidence and capacities to work and to build political awareness and knowledge. Presently total 1902 elected women representatives are part of 816 taluka level Panchayati Raj Women's Front.

SECTION-IV
IMPACT AND CHALLENGES

The impact of MRA process is visible at various levels. First and foremost upon the women who have been actively involved in MRA processes at the village and other levels. Active village level units have been able to take up several local concerns and thus impact can be seen on women's collective level. Inputs and support to EWRs and their organisation building has led to changes in the local decision-making processes and Gram Panahcyat functioning.

Impact at individual level among MRA members—MRA has succeeded in developing leadership abilities of its members. Exposure and capacity building through various activities has led to enhanced understanding, positive attitude and sense of solidarity among the women. Thus, empowerment is visible in terms of:

- Increased self-confidence and self-esteem in EWRs and rural women.
- Increased leadership qualities.
- Greater acceptance to women as leaders in the society.
- Improved status in family and society.
- Increased awareness and motivation level of EWRs.

Impact at panchayat/governance level—Informed and active participation of MRA members in Gram Panchayat functioning has led to changing existing stereotypes. Pro-people approach and transparent functioning is integral in executing development work through various government schemes. Impact is also visible at the level of Gram Sábha/Mahila Sabha and these public forums have been activated. Most importantly emphasis on value based politics is reflected in day to day functioning. The changed nature of panchayat functioning can be seen in terms of:

- Increased social accountability and transparency in the local village affairs.
- Successful implementation of government schemes by the EWRs like Gadge Maharaj Village Cleanliness Campaign, Indira Awas Yojana, Public Distribution System, Antyodaya Scheme, Sanjay Gandhi Niradhar Yojana, Employment Guarantee Yojana, Pradhan Mantri Gram Sadak Yojana, etc.
- Using PRIs to address a variety of issues affecting women – Rape, Sexual Harassment, dowry, inadequacies of Government structures.

Impact at the level of women's collectives – The process of empowerment is not limited to governance issues alone and can also be seen in addressing strategic gender issues. On various occasion MRA has taken up issues like household work, right to property and joint ownership of household and also made efforts to bring alcohol abuse and domestic violence onto the agendas of political campaigns. Conscious attempts have been made to sensitise and involve men as partners in the social change process. Impact of MRA work on women's collectives can be seen in various areas, such as:

- SHGs acting as a base for uniting women for mass actions.
- Strengthening of women SHGs.
- Challenging patriarchal—stereotypical roles of women.
- Challenging the established traditional power centres.
- Collective ownership towards the issues of development.
- Good knowledge of social issues and comprehending their inter linkages.
- Good Rapport with various stakeholders.
- Increasing understanding about caste-class-gender power relations.
- Priorities of development in favour of the venerable – women, Dalits and tribal.
- Dalit women emerging as active, with strong leadership qualities.

Impact at the policy level – In order to create an enabling policy environment MRA has consistently raised critical demands and succeeded in making positive changes at the policy levels. These include:

- Conferring of effective powers to Gram Sabha, December 2002.
- Mandatory Women's Gram Sabhas.
- State Government has accepted MRAs' demand to make suitable amendments to resolve the issue of suspended Gram Sabha.
- BDOs are advised to give adequate publicity to Taluka meetings to ensure participation by women.
- Three-fourth majority is made mandatory to unseat women Sarpanch through No-confidence motion, thus putting a check on improper and gender biased use of statutory provisions.
- State Government has agreed to implement Gram Sevikas on experimental basis.
- Ten per cent Budget for women to be implemented rigorously.
- Priority given to Mahila Mandals for allocation of land by the Government committees is to be extended to other committees as well.
- A Resolution stating that Flag hoisting should necessarily be done by the Elected Women Sarpanchs.

Challenges

Though tangible gains have been made at various levels, as presented above, MRA still faces critical challenges. There is always a possibility of backlash whenever women assert themselves. Women's collective action faces severe reaction in terms of verbal and physical abuse. Such instances are ample, although very few become known. This is the fourth phase Panchayati Raj in Maharashtra and the nature of challenges has changed over the period. Some of the major challenges before the Elected Women Representatives (EWRs) include:

- Pressure to stick back to traditional roles.

- Increased expectations of the people to make changes and prove ones' capabilities.
- Lack of co-operation from men from community and administration.
- Pressure from political parties.
- Value-less politics muddled with corruption, alcohol liquor, and muscle power.
- Changing political, societal, cultural and economic scenario due to onslaught of globalisation, privatisation, liberalisation.
- Lack of resources and livelihood means for disadvantaged and discriminated sections.
- Clearly these challenges demand invigorated collective action. In this context, MRA is planning to sustain the collective processes already set in place and strengthen them by accommodating new actors in the social change process. For instance, MRA is planning to involve rural youth in their programmes and to form a youth front which will work hand in hand with other MRA fronts.

SECTION-V
WAY AHEAD

Mahila Rajsatta Andolan (MRA), in particular, has planned campaigns to widely propagate MRA ideology (MRA Manifesto Awareness Campaign) to sensitise men (Jotiba Jagruti Abhiyan). MRA plans to strengthen Panchayati Raj Women's Front by increasing membership and enhancing specific capacities like budget planning and utilisation.

One of the ambitious plan of MRA is setting up of Savitribai Phule Political Academy, which will be an institute offering need-based courses for EWRs for knowledge and perspective building.

At the policy level, MRA plans to pursue execution of travel concession to women Sarpanchs in state transport, which would particularly help Sarpanch from marginalised and poor sections of the society. MRA also supports demand for special Act to provide protection to EWRs against violence and one-third reservations to women in Parliament and Legislative Assemblies. Following precedent of Madhya Pradesh MRA would also like to push for 50 per cent reservations to women in local governing institutions.

The idea of Karbharni Fellowship is devised to raise sponsorship for elected women representatives. These ideas are still at a very nascent stage, however, certainly bear potential to widen resource and support base for the struggle spearheaded by the grassroots women leaders.

(*Source*: Mahila Rajsatta Andolan Mra mahila_rajsatta@yahoo.com)

2

Formation and Strengthening of Panchayat Elected Women Representatives Networks in Andhra Pradesh

An Empowerment Strategy

C. Vijaya Shyamala

Introduction

The one-third reservation to the women in PRIs through the 73rd Constitutional Amendment has undoubtedly created space for the vast number of women in the political decision-making processes at the grassroots level. According to Susheela Kaushik[1] "this is, indeed, a unique experiment in the world of democracy, wherein women at grassroots level, irrespective of their educational, professional and socio-economic background, have been found suitable enough to occupy political positions and participate in legislating, decision-making and governance."

Reservation has brought in much promise not only for the "empowerment" of women but also for "cleansing" the vitiated political system. Firstly, participation in political institutions i.e., making of policies and decisions and an effective control in getting them implemented has the potential to empower women and promote equality and justice. Representation of women in large numbers in these institutions is intended to promote or stimulate democratisation of politics. This enlarges possibilities for women to be better integrated in the political processes. It is also expected that this power will enable them to address women's issues and influence decisions, which in turn will lead to an enhancement of their status and thereby weaken patriarchy paving the way towards greater equality. Secondly, Shri Rajiv Gandhi, the visionary of the 73rd Amendment believed that presence of women in large numbers in the Panchayats will not only make the Panchayats more representative but will also make them more efficient, honest, disciplined and more responsible because traditionally financial discipline and fiscal responsibility are ingrained in the habits and outlook of the women of rural India, qualities badly needed in Panchayati Raj Institutions (PRIs).

The Andhra Pradesh Panchayati Raj Act, 1994, passed in conformity with the 73rd Constitutional Amendment Act has provided the one-third reservation to women in all the positions at all levels of the PRIs. Since then three elections were held to the PRIs in 1995, 2001 and 2006 and with rotation system the three terms have provided entry to a large number of women elected representatives.

One positive outcome of reservation is the space provided to the women in the hitherto male dominated grassroot decision-making bodies. The experience indicates that initially women occupied only the reserved seats that too with reluctance and pressure from the males, presently women are contesting in the open seats, some even as independents and getting elected in more number than the 33 per cent which is a clear indication of the women showing interest to push themselves into the system despite all its odds. The other positive outcomes have been affiliations with the political parties, upward political mobility for few and an imptovement in the social and economic status (may be temporary and non-sustainable).

A deeper analysis, however, indicates that these overt achievements need not be glorified to the extent of being complacent or ignore the latent concerns of the majority of the women elected representatives. The various constraints faced by all the women representatives, instances of exploitation, harassment and violence are issues of major concern and have to be viewed and debated in the larger perspective of the deep-rooted patriarchy which is all pervasive and the major cause for the majority women not being to be able to perform effectively or independently. Thus, the empowerment of women elected representatives towards realising the objectives of reservation requires not only measures like capacity building programmes, gender budgeting, proactive state and bureaucracy but also a convergent women empowerment strategy involving economic and social factors.

The Empowerment Strategy

The term "Empowerment", although defined variously, is a participatory process and involves various mutually reinforcing aspects like access to resources, knowledge and awareness, developing skills and capacity building, greater participation, decision-making power, and gaining control.

UNICEF has developed the Women's Empowerment Framework[2] according to which women's development can be viewed in terms of five levels of equality, of which empowerment is an essential element at each level. The five levels are:

(i) *Welfare,* the first level, addresses only the basic needs of women, without recognising or attempting to solve the underlying structural causes, which necessitate provision of welfare services. At this point, women are merely passive beneficiaries of welfare benefits.

(ii) *Access,* the second level, is essential for women to make meaningful progress. This involves equality of access to resources, such as education opportunities, land and credit. The path to empowerment is initiated when women recognise their lack of access to resources as a barrier to their growth and overall well-being, and take action to address this.

(iii) *Conscientisation* is a crucial point in the Empowerment framework. For women to take appropriate action to close gender gaps or gender inequalities, there must be recognition that their problems stem from inherent structural and institutional discrimination. They must also recognise the role they can often play in reinforcing the system that restricts their growth.

(iv) *Participation* is the point where women are taking decisions alongside men equally. To reach this level, however, mobilisation is necessary. By organising themselves and working collectively, women will be empowered to gain increased representation, which will lead to increased empowerment and ultimately greater control.

(v) *Control,* is the ultimate level of equality and empowerment. Here, the balances of power between men and women are equal and neither party has dominance over the other. At this stage women are able to make decisions over their lives, and the lives of their children, and play an active role in the development process. Further, the contributions of women are fully recognised.

As women move gradually upward from welfare (the lowest level) to control (the highest level), increased empowerment enable them to understand the nature of gender subordination, critically challenge it and creatively reshape their own world. The above empowerment framework is widely accepted and any programme or project aimed at empowering women can be analysed by using it.

If the above framework is applied to women representatives in PRIs, one-third reservation of all the seats can be considered to be the first level, i.e., a welfare measure to address the absence of women in adequate numbers in the decision-making bodies. The existing status of women representatives at the end of three terms of reservation in Andhra Pradesh clearly reveals that they have a long way to go before they achieve the final stage i.e., Control wherein women are able to make decisions over their lives, and the lives of their children, and play an active role in the development process.

The three stages in between—access to resources, conscientisation and participation, have to be addressed simultaneously for the empowerment process to be quick and complete. Access to resources and equal opportunities (roots in patriarchy), particularly economic is a major constraint for women's participation and this has to be addressed by conscientisation of women to these gender inequalities, lack of access to resources and the role they need to play to overcome these hindrances. The women need to not only be aware of their constraints and the root cause but also participate in the making of decisions that affect their lives and the overall development of which they are a part. While participating, women need to possess the necessary information and knowledge to articulate their views, put strong pressure for their views to be accepted and implemented.

Experience has proved that, with regard to participation, women elected representatives are broadly of two categories—First, who are passive allowing their male members to act on their behalf. Second, who are trying to perform on their own but in the process facing a lot of hurdles like male domination, apathy and non-cooperation of officials, to the extent of disempowerment. Both the categories need courage and support to do justice to their positions and the achievement of the objectives of reservation. Collectives or Networks provide the strength to draw inspiration and courage from each other to fight for any injustice to individuals and also act as pressure groups to bring about the structural and institutional changes required for their empowerment. Thus, the empowerment strategy should essentially involve building networks of elected women representatives in addition to the trainings and awareness generation programmes.

Formation of Networks of Elected Women Representatives

The Context

In Andhra Pradesh, the Sarpanches have, on their own initiative, come together in 1995 and formed the Andhra Pradesh Sarpanches Association to address certain pressing issues of Sarpanches. Similarly, the MPTCs also came together in 2004 to address the issues of MPTCs.

The point to be made is that both these associations had few women members participating and never in the agenda were the issues pertaining to women elected members.

CWS, in its operational areas, as a part of its interventions, initially facilitated formation of exclusive networks of SCs, Sarpanches, Ward Members etc. but with experience gained, later changed the strategy and facilitated formation of one Network of All PR leaders with 50 per cent representation to women and also exclusive network of Elected Women Representatives from all levels. The initiatives of CWS are, however, limited to its operation area of 9 mandals spread over 8 districts in Andhra Pradesh.

In 2007, CWS was identified as nodal agency to implement the MoPR, GoI's Panchayat Mahila Evam Yuva Shakti Abhiyan (PMEYSA) programme in AP, the objective of which is empowerment of elected women representatives through trainings, district/divisional level sammelans and formation of networks.

The experience of CWS in facilitating the Panchayat Elected Women Representatives (EWRs) Federation under the PMEYSA is presented in this chapter.

Panchayat Mahila Evam Yuva Shakti Abhiyan (PMEYSA)

In order to address the empowerment of EWRs and Elected Youth Representatives (EYRs) in a systematic, programmatic manner and not rely on *ad hoc* and sporadic interventions, the Ministry of Panchayati Raj, Government of India, launched a scheme entitled the **Panchayat Mahila Evam Yuva Shakti Abhiyan** in the year 2006 and Center for World Solidarity was identified as nodal agency for implementing the programme in AP by the Commissioner, Panchayati Raj, Government of Andhra Pradesh in 2007.

The objective of the programme is to enable women and youth Panchayat leaders to come together to articulate their problems, discuss issues regarding the institutional mechanisms for their empowerment, come up with a charter of issues to be mainstreamed into policy and advocacy support so that their concerns are addressed by the process of development adopted by the State and the three-tier PRI system, and form an association of the EWRs with elected office bearers and with cascading representation of EWRs from the district level and divisional level EWRs organisations.

PMEYSA Guidelines for the Formation of State Association

A State level Sammelan will be organised in each State where the elected women representatives will assemble together for 2-3 days to debate, discuss and deliberate on the issues that affect them as Panchayati Raj Representatives. The sammelan would be a residential event in each State wherein all the EWRs (Zilla Pramukhs, Panchayat Samiti Pradhans and at least 5-10 women Sarpanchs) from every district of the State will be represented. The initial day would be reserved for women sarpanchs from districts to meet, gather and speak in an atmosphere of informality and warmth. On the second day, the group will be joined by women Pradhans (Panchayat Samiti) and Women Zilla Pramukhs who will join together to finalise the draft charter of EWRs of the State.

One of the major outcomes of the State level Sammelan is the formation of the State level Association with elected office bearers amongst the EWRs. Due representation will be given to women belonging to SCs/STs/OBCs in the Executive/Management Committees of the Association.

There will be an elected Executive Body of the EWR Association, elected during the sammelan, or just subsequent to it, which may register itself, decide on its institutional form, charge membership fees, and decide on the detailed activities which it may undertake in order to fulfil its mandate. The Executive Body of the Association will also prepare a structure for the Association e.g., State Management Committee, Divisional and District Committees, etc. and mentor the same.

The above Committees are not parallel bodies/committees to undermine the functioning of the Panchayati Raj Institutions. The State, Division and District Level Committees mentioned above will facilitate the creation of a network of Elected Women Representatives who would improve the functioning and viability of Panchayati Raj Institutions (PRIs) through their influence and vantage position over policy decisions. The objective is to create a forum where the EWRs can freely talk about issues faced by them as elected representatives, which will in turn enable them to voice their ideas, concerns and priorities in the local panchayat meetings with greater efficiency and to use the strength of the women collectives to improve gender relations within family and society as also increase the bargaining power of the EWRs. Since, the Panchayats have to be actively engaged in local level plan formulation and implementation, discussions on alternative development models on gender, etc. will help the EWRs to be creatively engaged in discussions and decision-making. The effort is to create a broad based leadership of women at the Panchayat level for the success and efficacy of democracy at the village level.

Role of the Association

- To raise the collective voice of EWRs against gender injustice, child exploitation, untouchability, land alienation and acquisition, encroachments, etc. and other relevant issues.
- To forward the resolutions passed by the EWR Association to the State government for necessary action.
- Participate in seminars organised by the State government or other agencies and disseminate the knowledge therein.
- Prepare action plans to strengthen the Association including the process of election of the Association for democratic participation of the EWRs.
- Provide knowledge support to the EWRs as well as handholding support as and when required through the State Support Centres. The Association would hire some minimal knowledge support workers who can fill the knowledge and information gap for EWRs when they require the same, help trouble shoot, help as resource persons and provide information on attendant issues like free legal aid, accounts and record keeping support, techniques of social audit, etc.
- The Executive Body of the Association will also manage the State Support Centres with the support of and experience of persons from the open market and implementing voluntary organisations as well as the NYKS and Youth Associations.

The Process of Formation of State Level Association by CWS

The Andhra Pradesh State-level Sammelan of women elected representatives under the PMEYSA was held on the 28th and 29th January, 2008. In the two day meeting, a total of about 500 elected women representatives discussed, deliberated and came up with a charter of demands which was presented to the Hon'ble Union Minister for Panchayati Raj, Shri Mani Shankar Aiyyar. Another important outcome proposed is the formation of State Level Association. However, the core committee members of the PMEYSA discussed and resolved that the Association should evolve from below and not formed directly and hastily during the Sammelan. It was, therefore, decided to decentralise the process of election to each district and the following modalities have been worked out for formation of Association:

- In each district, the Zilla Parishad Chairperson (male/female) will take the lead role and participatorily identify seven active members comprising of one woman ZP chairperson/vice chairperson/ZPTC, one woman MPP, one woman MPTC, 2 women Sarpanlchs and 2 women Ward Members.
- Total of one hundred and fifty-four (7 × 22 districts) will form the electoral college and meet at the state level and elect the Association.

The process of formation of State Level Association was initiated in the month of February 2008 requesting the ZP chairpersons of all the 22 districts in AP to identify a 7 member district committee of active EWRs representing different levels, castes and parties. There was response from 16 districts nominating 7 members as per the criterion. The electoral college of 114 elected women representatives were called for a meeting at Hyderabad on the 1st March, 2008 to elect the Executive Body of the state level association. During the meeting the 7 Members of each district committee discussed amongst themselves and sent one to represent their district in the State body. The Association was thus initially formed with 16 members representing 16 districts. Each of the 16 members were asked to speak about themselves and their performance. The Chairperson, Vice Chairperson, Secretary and Treasurer were then nominated based on their education, articulation capabilities and achievements. Subsequently, the representatives from the balance 6 districts were identified through follow up with the local NGOs and contacts of the other members of the State body. The background details of the members of Association are shown in Annexure-1.

Strengthening of the State Association and District Committees

Initially in 2007 funds were released only for the Conducting of the State Level Sammelan, the first step in the process. After successfully organising the Sammelan in January 2008 and formation of State Level Association in March 2008, CWS submitted the proposal for

2008-2009 as per the activities stipulated in the guidelines. The budget sanctioned for the State Level Association was Rs. 25,000.

Setting up a State Support Centre (SSC) with three staff members to coordinate the activities of PMEYSA, serve as a knowledge support centre and ultimately be managed by the State Association is one envisaged activity under PMEYSA. The SSC was set up and a launching ceremony was organised on 21st July, 2008, by inviting all the 22 association members and the Commissioner, Panchayati Raj as the chief guest. A total of 80 participants including 16 members of State Association, members of Core Committee, Staff of CWS and other special invitees attended. The Association members had a meeting after the inauguration and discussed about the Registration and resolved to register under the Societies Act of AP.

Process of Registration of State Association

- Draft By-Laws Prepared by convener and SSC staff and required documents produced in the registration office.
- Registrar requested for a letter from the government endorsing that the Association is formed as per the guidelines of PMEYSA.
- MoPR obliged and sent us an endorsement letter.
- The entire process took almost 6 months.
- The registration no. of the elected women representatives 21 of 2009 and registered as "The Andhra Pradesh Panchayat Elected Women Representatives Association".

Since the budget for State Level Association is meager, the members were facilitated to attend the 5 divisional (four to five districts) level meetings organised at Hyderabad, Guntur, Ananthapur, Vishakapatnam and Warangal. This gave a good exposure to the members, a sense of recognition, opportunity to learn from the input sessions and also helped develop a comraderie among the members. Simultaneously, the association had its meetings and discussed about strategies for strengthening the State level body and building networks from mandal level with organic linkages. However, the constraint faced was that despite facilitation by the SSC staff and travel costs and other logistics taken care, the members attending these divisional level meetings was very low.

Another exclusive meeting of the executive committee was facilitated on the May 12th, 2009 at St Ann's Generelate, Tarnaka, which was attended by 8 out of the total 22 members. The members discussed at detail on the low attendance and agreed to take up the responsibility themselves of contacting other members of neighbouring districts. It was also discussed that a member being regularly absent will be asked whether she is interested or not and replaced by someone else. In this meeting the Structure for the Federation (Annexure-2) was worked out by the members. The members also expressed that district level meetings in their respective districts would be useful in strengthening the district committees and also bringing larger number into the fold of the PMEYSA.

As a process of strengthening the Association, the members of state association and the district committees are involved along with the local NGOs in the sensitisation training programmes organised in their respective districts.

The proposal for 2009-2010 was submitted to the MoPR through the State Government in July 2009. The funds, however, were released only in April 2010. Meanwhile, the state training institute APARD extended some support to strengthen the State Association. Two meetings of the State Association were held with APARD providing the meeting hall, accommodation and food for the participants and the travel was taken care by CWS. The district committees could not be strengthened because there was no budget provided for their meetings. However, the members still identify themselves as district committee.

As suggested by the members in the May 12th meeting, it was proposed to organise District level meetings in 6 districts. After the release of funds in April 2010, a review and planning meeting was held on 16th April with the members of State Association. The members discussed the sanctioned budget and the proposed activities and came out with the following decisions:

1. The 6 District Level meetings will be organised in Mahbubnagar, Guntur, Prakasam, Anantapur, Khammam and Kadapa.
2. The objective will be to provide a platform for about 150 women representatives and form the district committee,

as per the proposed structure, with one representative from each LAC (Legislative Assembly Constituency area) and nominate point persons for each mandal in the district to take up the responsibility of forming the Mandal Committees.

3. The sensitisation trainings proposed for 66 batches will be spread over the 22 districts with 3 batches and the concerned member of the Association will identify the local NGOs and conduct them with the overall coordination and guidance from the staff of SSC.

As per the action plan and the decisions taken, 15 sensitisation trainings in 5 districts are completed with active involvement of the respective members of State Association. One district level meeting is completed in Mahbubnagar. The meeting was entirely conducted under the leadership of Ms. Aruna, Vice President of the Association. A total of 150 women representatives from about 58 mandals out of the total 64 mandals participated. Inputs were provided on Gender issues, Leadership skills and networking. One representative for each of the 14 LACs were elected from amongst the participants and formed into a district committee. Point persons for the 58 mandals were identified. The entire meeting organised by the Women Elected Representatives themselves under the leadership of Ms. Aruna was very inspiring to others. She could mobilise the participation of two Ministers, one MLA, and one ex-MLA, Chairperson, ZPP, who all lauded the programme and its objectives and promised support. The other members of the Association who attended the meeting got an exposure and also inspiration to make it a success in their districts too.

The latest in the process of strengthening State Association is a three day programme in Hyderabad. Day one had input sessions on Communication skills, Conflict resolution, Leadership and Gender concepts and Acts. Day two was utilised for the brainstorming of the strategies for further strengthening the Association. On the third day, the members of the Association met the Honourable Minister for Panchayati Raj and the Commissioner, Panchayati Raj and expressed their various concerns and gave a representation for the following:

- Extend the Reservation to second term to consolidate the experience of the Women Representatives.

- To enhance the Women Reservation from the present 33 per cent to 50 per cent.
- To lift the ban on Treasury and to release funds to Mandal and Panchayat level.
- To appoint the President/Executive at each Panchayat level for administrative support
- Devolution of Powers, Funds and Functionaries to PRIs.
- Appoint special staff for the purpose of water and sanitation.

Achievements

1. After two years of consistent efforts for strengthening, 15 members out of the 22 are now strong and committed to take forward the Association with their developed leadership qualities. These women will complete their term in another eight months. However, they have expressed their interest in continuing to be associated and guide the newcomers.
2. The association has initiated the advocacy efforts with the Government.
3. The Members, in their respective districts, are responding to the women's issues.
4. The Members are actively taking the responsibility for the sensitisation trainings in their respective districts, coordinating with the local NGOs and also participating in them. In the process they are getting more exposure through interactions with fellow women representatives, at the same time sharing of their experiences and learnings through PMEYSA is projecting them as Role Models.

Constraints

1. The association has not been formed out of the self-initiative of the EWRs. It is formed by the facilitation of an NGO as a programme with funds from the Central Government. Thus, despite meeting all their travel and lodging costs, a lot of facilitation had to be done to bring them to the meetings and sustain their interest. Although many of the members have now realised the importance of networking and

Association, still a sense of ownership and collective leadership has to be developed.

2. Since it is a government programme, the implementation is constrained by the guidelines, inadequate budget for the Association strengthening *per se*, lack of flexibility in making adjustments in the different budget heads, delays in the release of amounts etc.

Challenges Ahead

- Promoting networks at mandal level and district level with linkages up to State level in 6 districts this year and subsequently in other 16 districts phase-wise. It is a slow and long term process requiring continuous facilitation to sustain the State level Association and developing the linkages from networks below.
- Adequate, continuous and timely budget required for sustaining the momentum. Other sources of funding and linkages for collaboration with likeminded organisations have to be developed.
- Develop the capacities to address women, child and youth issues at their respective levels addressing through networks.
- Model Women leaders developed for encouraging and inspiring others.

Conclusion

Although, the formation of networks by EWRs themselves on their own initiative is an ideal situation, as discussed in the beginning, in the empowerment framework they are at welfare level. To reach the control level, they have to be conscientised and collectivised which is also the aim of PMEYSA.

In Andhra Pradesh, Sarpanchs Association and MPTCs Associations are formed without outside facilitation and although they are Registered and continuing to exist, the onus of sustaining them is entirely on few individual leaders who are spending their own money to run the show. These Associations have also failed to give adequate representation to EWRs or address their specific issues. In AP with

Rotation system, most of the EWRs are first timers with no experience and exposure and majority are dependent on male support. Despite facilitation, meeting all the expenses etc., EWRs have constraints in attending the network meetings. In this context, despite the constraints in implementation, the need to facilitate to bring them together, educate and network so as to address their concerns is very crucial until some strong leaders are developed with the capacities to network on their own even when there is no external support.

The PMEYSA is a good concept and can be utilised to outreach to a larger number of EWRs which in other cases is difficult. A few Role Model EWRs developed in the process will itself be a great achievement.

Annexure–I

Details of the Executive Committee Members of State Level Association

Sl. No	District	Name	Position	Designation	Age	Education	Term	Party
1	Guntur	Ms. Vijaya	Chairperson	Z.P.T.C. Chairperson	45	MSc., M.Phil	First	Congress
2	Mahboobnagar	Ms. Aruna	Vice President	M.P.P	35	M.A.B.Ed.	First	Congress
3	Prakasam	Ms. Narsamma	Secretary	M.P.P	50	B.A.	First	Congress
4	Ranga Reddy	Ms. Parijatha	Jt. Secreatry	Surpanch	28	B.A.	First	Congress
5	Khammam	Ms. Eswari Bai	Treasurer	Surpanch	32	B.A.	First	Congress
6	Medek	Ms. Sudha Rani	Member	Surpanch	55	SSC	First	TDP
7	Kadapa	Ms. Sailaja	Member	M.P.P	29	B.Com.	First	Congress
8	Nizamabad	Ms. Godavari	Member	MPTC	38	Inter	First	Congress
9	East Godavari	Ms. Vanisri Devi	Member	Ward Member	36	10th Class	First	TDP
10	Nellore	Ms. Anitha	Member	Z.P.T.C.	37	Dip. Eng.	Second	Congress
11	Vijayanagaram	Ms. Jyothi	Member	Surpanch	43	Inter	Second	TDP
12	Karimnagar	Ms. Komala	Member	Surpanch	27	B.A.	First	TDP
13	Srikakulam	Ms. Gajalaxmi	Member	Surpanch	43	Inter	First	Congress
14	West Godavari	Ms. Nagamani	Member	Surpanch	40	Inter	First	Congress
15	Ananthapur	Ms. Laxmi Devamma	Member	Surpanch	38	5th Class	First	TDP
16	Adilabad	Ms. Tanubai	Member	Surpanch	46	5th Class	First	Congress
17	Nalgonda	Ms. Neelam Padma	Member	Z.P.T.C.	35	B.A.	First	Congress
18	Kurnool	Ms. Shesi Rekha	Member	M.P.P	37	B.A.	First	Congress
19	Warangal	Not attending meetings and efforts on to identify new members in these 4 districts						
20	Chittor							
21	Vishakapatnam							
22	Krishna							

Annexure–II

Structure of Federation

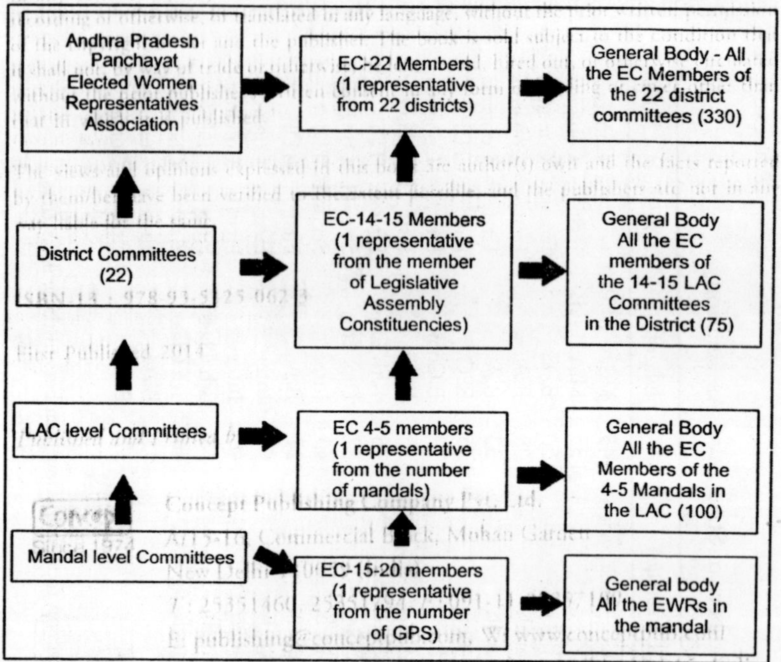

NOTES

1. National Commission for Women, 2001, "Participation of Women in Panchayati Raj in India, A Stock Taking, New Delhi, pp. iii.
2. UNICEF, "The Women's Empowerment Framework", *Women and Girls Advance*, vol. 1, No. 1, 1993, p. 5.

3

Panchayat Mahila Manch – Gujarat

Mahila Swaraj Abhiyan

Avani Rawal

Context

In the year 1993, the implementation of 73rd Constitutional Amendment Act (CAA) heralded a new era in the participation of Indian women and marginalised populations in Local Self-Governance Institutions (LSGI). With the implementation of this CAA, 33 per cent of all seats in LSGIs were reserved for women. In a country where women have been kept out of power for hundreds and thousands of years, women's participation in governance and in political life has been nominal. The CAA laid the way for a paradigm shift in participation of women in local governance in our country.

The Working Group for Women Issues in Gujarat (WGWI-G) emerged during this time, with the aim of working on women's issues including the double burden of work, atrocities faced by women in society, and in their families, as well as class/caste/religious discrimination. Issues identified specifically for women entering the political sphere included a lack of awareness about mechanisms available to them in both public and political institutions, lack of awareness about their rights and responsibilities, and a lack of women role models in political life. Grassroots women expressed fears and anxieties about their capability and capacity to participate in and control the right to make decisions as elected representatives. In order to hear first-hand the issues faced by Elected Women Representatives (EWRs), in 1997 a Panchayat Behenon nu Milan (A State level event of EWRs) was organised by WGWI-G and many NGOs and CBOs working on women's concerns. Through this event the need for a forum for EWRs emerged—a place where EWRs could meet on a regular basis to share their experiences and concerns related to their participation in political life at the grassroots level. Women stated a need for guidance and support as they explored this foreign domain. EWRs expressed a need for efforts to increase their awareness, build their capacity as leaders and LSGI functionaries. This they felt would enable them individually as leaders elected by the people, and from that would stem a mass of EWRs, who would take their rightful places as leaders elected by their constituents.

Genesis

As EWRs' concerns came to light during the Panchayat Baheno nu Milan Mahila Swaraj Abhiyan (MSA) was formed, with the intent of highlight their concerns as related to good governance. Since its inception MSA has taken a lead in strategising, developing and implementing educational activities, research, training, media, networking events and advocacy campaigns to increase women's participation in LSGIs and facilitate the mainstreaming of gender in governance and LSGIs.

In the year 2000, through consultation and assessment of EWRs felt needs, MSA formulated the concept of Panchayat Mahila Manch (PMM). The PMM's objectives include the creation of a common platform where EWRs from LSGIs can share their personal experiences as EWRs, seek information about the inner workings of LSGIs, build their capacities to work as effective leaders, and develop strategies to address their, as well as local issues in front of local bureaucracy and administration.

This chapter describes the concept of PMM, our experiences of facilitating the PMMs over the past 8 years, experiences of PMM members as key players in the functioning of this enabling environment, put forward lessons learned and challenges which have arisen during the journey of PMMs in Gujarat.

Panchayat Mahila Manch: The Initial Years

An initial strategy of the PMM was to build capacity of EWRs to effectively perform their duties as elected representatives to LSGIs and create a space for the emergence of women leaders. The focus was on the provision of information, enhancing required skills, and providing support for first-timers in the political sphere, in order for them to practice good governance and do justice to their roles.

Through issue-identification and prioritisation, grassroots campaigns on drinking water and social security were designed and implemented through EWRs. These campaigns were envisioned to strategically mobilise EWRs, and create an identity for them in their immediate sphere of influence at the local level.

At the end of the campaign MSA and EWRs learned that by merely mobilising to addressing local issues through campaigns, EWRs were not moving through the process of self-empowerment, nor were they building their capacities to participate in, and affect the wider political process.

Mahila Swaraj Abhiyan (MSA) with EWRs then visualised the PMMs as a forum where a mass of EWRs could come together at one place and time, to develop strategies that can affect local issues, link them with workings at the higher levels of bureaucracy and government administration, address EWRs concerns as a mass, as well as enhance the efficient functioning of LSGIs. Here they could also rely on the strength of numbers, when making demands in the political sphere.

A Demonstration Model

Establishing a collective responsibility, MSA with grassroots CBOs and NGOs came together to mobilise EWRs. Following their mobilisation, it was envisioned that these partner civil society organisations would support EWRs' full functioning as effective leaders and monitor their governance capacities. When the second round of rural LSGI elections was anticipated, MSA worked with its member and partner CBOs and NGOs to design demonstration models which would be directly undertaken in several districts of Gujarat. By design, MSA's partner CBOs and member NGOs would build their own knowledge about LSGIs, mobilise and facilitate the functioning of a new cadre of EWRs, and continue to undertake their mandated work through locally elected functionaries especially EWRs.

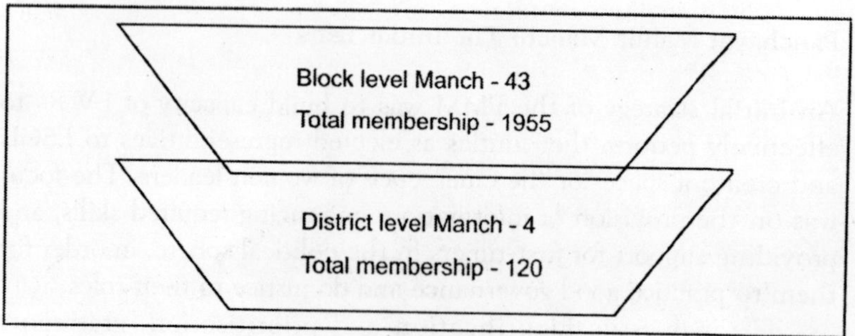

Fig. 3.1: Demonstration Model.

These demonstration models presently exist at the Block and District levels in six districts of Gujarat. In Dahod, Panchmahal, Sabarkantha and Surendranagar districts, MSA has designed PMMs as demonstration models, where experimenting, re-formulations, learning and re-strategising are the modus operandi. Two of MSA's network members and founders from the time of the PBM in 1997, Kutch Mahila Vikas Sangathan (KMVS) and Anandi, have adopted the model and initiated block level PMMs in two other districts of Gujarat, Kutch and Bhavnagar.

Objectives and Membership

Since their inception, PMMs have struggled to facilitate the empowerment of EWRs by supporting the recognition of their agency, legitimising their competence, providing necessary information with which to make conscious strategic decisions. Through the PMMs, MSA envisioned the creation of identities for member EWRs as effective leaders, and the conception of an identity for PMMs as a pressure body to monitor and hold government accountable for equitable development at the grassroots. To accomplish these goals, PMMs adopted the following objectives:

- Identify and affect gaps in gender-sensitivity of local governance functions and functionaries.

- Identify and carry forward the needs and concerns of EWRs, which affect their full functioning as effective leaders in LSGIs.
- Identify and affect development issues for women and marginalised populations, towards legitimising their political voice.

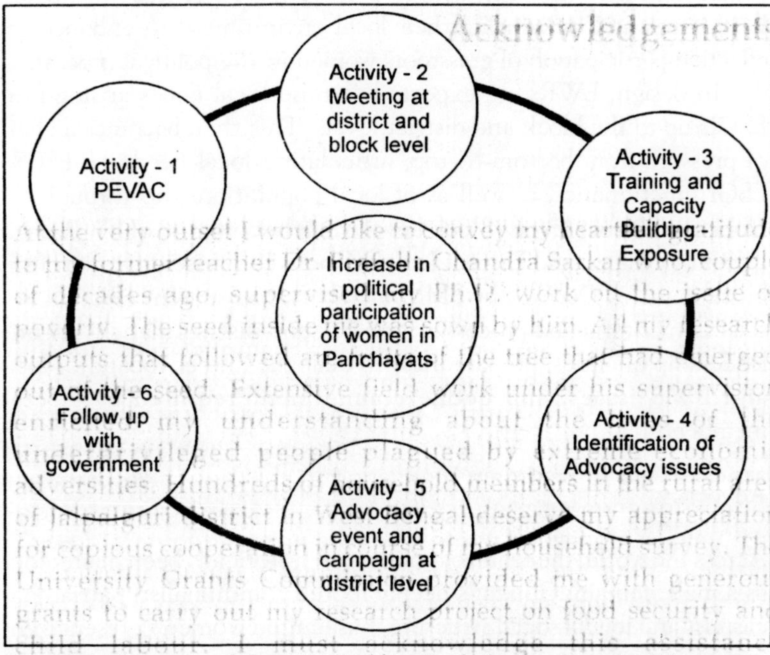

Fig. 3.2: Advocacy and Capacity Building Cycle for Panchayat Mahila Manch.

In order to achieve these objectives, Panchayat Mahila Manch (PMM) membership and their relationship with local institutions is crucial. At present, on average half of the membership in PMMs are EWRs, and the other half are members from SHGs, federations, former representatives, and other local women leaders. Within the group of EWRs, there is diversity, ranging from women who are genuine participants in the political process, to those who function as proxies for their families or other local influencing individuals. Some women come with political ambitions, some come to explore the new political environment and public life, and some come under duress. Diversity of membership in terms of levels of social-demographic self-confidence, awareness, agency, empowerment, has affected the speed and level at which the PMM has been able to prepare EWRs as leaders affecting local issues and influencing their local environment to enhance the effective participation of grassroots women in the political process.

In design, EWRs are expected to raise local issues arising from LSGIs up to the block and district levels. This then becomes a chain of pressure from bottom-to-top, articulating local needs, of EWRs, LSGI functionaries, as well as of local populations, up through the block and district levels. Block Level Manchs comprise of EWRs from different villages, and District Level Manchs comprises of leaders from block manchs. Decided by PMM members, transparent election and selection criteria and processes for block and district manchs ensures leadership qualities, preparedness to dialogue and advocate for local and EWR issues, and define commitment required by elected members.

Advocacy

Across the world, the realm of politics has historically been maintained as a male domain. Gujarat's deeply rooted communalist, patriarchal, casteist and feudal social structure, has limited women's presence and active participation in local politics. Reservations in the past 15 years have forced a rise in the visibility of women in LSGIs. However, there has been limited success in facilitating their active involvement in and contribution to decision-making in local government.

Within this restrictive and limiting environment PMM provides an avenue for EWRs to come together in a conducive environment, outside the holds of caste and religion, beyond vested interests of those in power. PMMs are established especially to facilitate EWRs' effective functioning as local leaders, and participation in local policy issues. From their inception, PMMs' membership has identified local policy advocacy issues through sharing and exchanges of experience in manch meetings held at block and district levels. Local advocacy issues address factors which limit EWRs' effective functioning at the local level, struggles to establish their credibility and legitimacy as leaders, and their acceptance as competent administrators and decision-makers in LSGI. Gender-sensitive good governance at the grassroots level sets the stage for accountable governance by EWRs at all levels. PMM and its membership supports EWRs' efforts to hold local, block, district and ultimately state governments accountable for ensuring appropriate and effective participation of women at all levels, of decision-making and active involvement in political processes.

In addition to grassroots advocacy issues, PMMs have also identified policy advocacy issues including:

- Amendments to "No Confidence" procedures against elected representatives.
- Refusal to accept "Sarpanch Pati" as administrative and executive functionary in place of EWRs.
- Increasing honorarium and providing life insurance benefits for grassroots elected representatives.
- Abolition of the Two Child Norm, as criteria for ousting elected representatives from their position.
- Establishing an additional quorum criterion in Gram Sabhas, specifically for women.

These advocacy issues have been identified by MSA, previous EWRs and manch members from their experiences after the second round of post-CAA elections. EWRs elected in 2006 have, through their participation in the PMMs, been oriented to these policy advocacy issues, and regularly debate these issucs during PMM meetings. Block manch members initiated a campaign in their local areas, seeking support from LSGI members on EWRs advocacy issues. As anticipated in an environment not yet ready to recognised issues of EWRs, PMM members faced many difficulties in generating support from male member of the LSGIs, and from local populations. Several PMMs have taken their demands to local government authorities as individuals, and as a collective through the PMM. They have had their demands heard, and in many cases received acknowledgement and support to move their demands through local level bureaucracy.

Experience and Learning

Panchayat Mahila Manch (PMM) as a demonstration model has revealed the potential for EWRs to converge their energies and efforts into a collaborative *critical mass* acting as a pressure body affecting their ability to make meaningful change both within their local realities as well as for policy changes. It has demonstrated a need for such platforms where EWRs can share their experiences, and strategise for change.

Panchayat Mahila Manch (PMM) has provided a learning ground where elected and non-elected women can explore opportunities to actively participate in the political sphere, and build their credibility and legitimacy as competent leaders in society. Diversity of membership within the PMM has the potential to provide inspiration to women not yet in leadership position or not yet involved in the political sphere. Former EWRs have played the role of mentors to the existing batch of elected women leaders, and now women who have an interest or an ambition for political involvement have role models to emulate.

All institutions, policies and laws need mechanisms in place to ensure active involvement by members of society, enforcement of policies and laws, as capacity building to ensure effective functioning as institutions. Although women's participation has been mandated in LSGIs, these institutions have not created a nurturing or conducive environment for their involvement. Neither EWRs as a group, nor their support structures have sufficiently moved through the process of empowered to the point where they can make informed choices that will affect their involvement in political life.

Women's presence in Gujarat's Gram Sabhas is noteably low. Those that come do not or are not given space to participate equally in discussions and decision-making. Gram Sabhas are the foundation for the decentralisation of Democracy in India, where local populations can demand transparency and accountability from their elected leaders. PMM is now steering the vision of its members towards influencing the larger LSGI body, making it more responsive to local women's needs. PMM is also considering the establishment of non-formal linkages with local women's groups, CBOs and SHGs, in order to mobilise potential women leaders, as well as encourage their participation in Gram Sabhas. In this way, the scope for PMM members to affect local issues, mobilise women to come to public and political life, highlight EWRs issues and make demands for advocacy-based changes will grow along with their credibility and legitimacy as leaders.

PMM's struggle to affect policy changes continues. Block and District level PMMs now have to come together and build pressure on the state government to actualise changes. An active state-level women's manch is presently in the long-term vision of the block and district level PMMs. This state-level manch will aim to dialogue and build relationships with state level officials and decision-makers, and monitoring the process of implementing changes for many of the advocacy issues identified at the grassroots.

The next election heralds 50 per cent reservation for women in LSGIs. This will create a wider space for larger numbers of women to participate in political processes. The scope of PMM should increase to capacity building and enabling women to function effectively in local governance as well as undertake advocacy issues at local, block and district levels. Women leaders in higher proportion will automatically heighten the awareness within society about women's right to actively participate in the political sphere and their right to demand equitable distribution of power and resources. With increased societal awareness at every level, PMM can play a preparatory role in strengthening an enabling environment.

The journey for PMMs and their members has been long and difficult. They are young and their structure continues to evolve. Their effectiveness and impacts are small, yet relatively significant. In the past years, PMMs changed their capacity building and hand-holding mandate into political action. PMMs have seen notable outcomes through innovative processes to create and expand a political space for EWRs. PMMs are slowly influencing social change, strengthening the participation of women in democratic institutions in Gujarat, and deepening the discourse on democracy at the grassroots.

4

Formation of Elected Women Representatives Association in Tamil Nadu

An Experience Sharing*

G. UMA AND J. VANISHREE

The enactment of the 73rd Constitutional Amendment Act in India has created a significant change in the political life of rural women. 50 per cent reservation of seats in the rural local bodies for women has provided an opportunity for women to exercise political power for the socio-economic development of their area. This critical mass of women is expected to perform the critical function. Thereby, the process of development would take a new turn and women's participation in governance would produce far reaching implications in the lives of the people. The decentralisation process has opened up opportunities for women and other marginalised groups to influence the process of governance. This is the greatest experiment in the contemporary situation by transferring decision-making power to two million elected women local government representatives. The new dispensation has opened an opportunity for many women with different socio-economic backgrounds to climb up the ladder of power with different sets of limitations and disabilities. However,

* The authors are grateful to Ms.Kalpana, Social activist, Chennai for helping them to understand the process involved in the formation of EWRs association in Tamil Nadu

there are a variety of barriers to women hailing from marginalised sections exercising their powers[1]. Women's participation in politics cannot be isolated from their overall socio-economic status and the following factors in particular. Women usually do not have equal access with men to the means of participation, such as the enabling skills acquired through education and training or controlling means of production or access to the information media including the new communications technologies. They often do not have decision-making power within the household to translate into the public sphere in many developing countries. Their possessions, including land and other collateral are legally the property of their husbands, fathers or sons. For this very reason, they have not been able to overcome gender biases and other barriers that obstruct their access to political decision-making.

Really it is a challenge to work for the social, economic and political empowerment of women, particularly those from marginalised sections. No doubt it is necessary to work for the goal of empowering women for which the oppressive power of the existing gender relations is to be exposed and challenged[2]. Further, the gender relations have to be shaped[3]. There are many institutions and organisations working towards strengthening women leadership at grassroots for effective delivery of services and achieve gender equity and equality. This chapter deals with one such experiment emerged from the grassroots. This experiment was facilitated by Rajiv Gandhi Chair for Panchayati Raj Studies in Gandhigram Rural University, Human Rights Foundation (HRF), Chennai and individuals like Prof. G.Palanithurai and Ms. Kalpana.

After the first local body election in the year 1996 (in accordance with the newly enacted Tamil Nadu Panchayati Raj Act, 1994), Kalpana, Programme Officer, Human Rights Foundation, a Non-Governmental Organisation (NGO), Chennai, organised a meeting for the Elected Women Representatives of Thiruvarur District, where she asked President of the Anaikuppam Panchayat to form an Elected Women Representatives Association which would exclusively provide women to voice their problems and motivate them to work independently without fear. But she stated that, due to familial responsibility, she was not able to take up the idea of the formation of an association. The other Elected Women Representatives did not responding regarding association formation. Then Ms. Kalpana urged Ms. Ponni to raise her voice as a representative of all Elected Women Representatives. This sowed the seed in her mind.

Even before the enactment of Tamil Nadu Panchayats Act 1994, Kalpana worked with Fisher women in the few Coastal Panchayats in the outskirts of Chennai where she formed fisher women *Sangam.* This *Sangam* was organised to approach government offices to meet their basic amenities and for proper delivery of services. Fisher women through this *Sangam* solved the issues like irregular water supply, power cut, transportation, etc. The *Sangam* experience made Kalpana to travel entire state to train the women leaders to contest in the election when first local body election was announced in Tamil Nadu in the year 1996. This training was provided by HRF. Dr. N. Markandan, former Vice-Chancellor, Gandhigram Rural University and Mr. M.L. Das are part of the training team. The training focused on how to address the issues concerned with rural areas. Governance was the main focus of the training. After 1996 Local body election she found that women have understood the election process but they have to be oriented in the governance process as well. So with the help of HRF, Kalpana, Dr. N. Markandan and M.L. Das organised training at the district level and identified grassroots women leaders who are very vocal in articulating their problems and issues in governance. They have identified group of leaders who are vocal and foundation was laid for the formation of women leaders association. This association was further strengthened by organising state level workshop and the women leaders association started meeting officials and politicians regularly to put forth their demands and to perform their governance functions.

In the meantime, Ms. Jesurathnam from SNEHA, a non-governmental organisation organised Elected Women Representatives meet at Ramanathapuram with the help of District Administration. Ms. Jesumary, President of Michealpattinam Village Panchayat had problem with the Makiti Panchayat regarding land dispute. Makiti Panchayat President threatened her, to kill. She sorted out the land dispute and election dispute with the help of District Administration.

At the same time, Ms. Jesumary came to know about District Level Elected Women Representatives President meeting. She too attended. Like her, many women Panchayat Presidents narrated their problems in the meeting. Ms. Jesurathinam provided solution that women leaders could have a network, they can voice their concern in the network meeting and they can sort out their problems.

Both Ms. Jesumary and Ms. Ponnikailasam analysed each and every situation related to work and to raise their concerns against not only their Panchayat issues, but there of Elected Women Representatives who were all criticised by their male counterparts from home to public life. Then they formed the association along with the other members of Thiruvarur District.

Even though they had not fully involved themselves in the ideas of an association, Rajiv Gandhi Chair for Panchayati Raj Studies in Gandhigram Rural University provided continuous opportunity to analyse the problems faced by women representatives. Rajiv Gandhi Chair for Panchayati Raj Studies too suggested that the Elected Women Representatives had to have their own organisation to voice their grievances.

There are many institutions and organisations working towards strengthening women leadership at grassroots for effective delivery of services and achieve gender equity and equality. Rajiv Gandhi Chair for Panchayati Raj Studies is one such centre actively working towards the above goal.

Accordingly, the perspective was developed by the Rajiv Gandhi Chair for Panchayati Raj Studies, Gandhigram Rural University, to assist Elected Women Representatives to carry out their roles and responsibilities effectively. The assumption is that capacitated Elected Women Representatives will serve their constituents more effectively. The perspective has following objectives: (i) to build an alliance of women leaders; (ii) to conscientise them on the issues which affect the life of women; (iii) to orient them in the methods and nuances of tacking the problems; (iv) to build capacity of the elected women representatives; and, (v) to build a support structure for elected women representatives. Hence, capacity building exercise for the Elected Women Representatives and support structure creation for them are the two imperatives.

Capacity Building Exercise

The UNDP defines the concept as the abilities of individuals, institutions and societies to perform functions solve problems and set and achieve objectives in a sustainable manner. It is described as a process through which these abilities are strengthened, adopted, and maintained overtime mostly (but not exclusively) in the public sector, through learning and practical management at both individual and institutional levels. According to Human Development Report 1995: Gender and Development[4]. "In no society do women enjoy the same opportunities as men; and removing gender inequality has nothing to do with national income or wealth."

The Beijing Platform for Action embodies two strategic objectives ensuring women's equal access to and full participation in power structures and decision-making; and increasing women's capacity to participate in decision-making and leadership.

Increased and more systematic formal and informal training is needed to increase the effectiveness of women's political knowledge and skills, as well as their capacity to utilise the emerging gender equity knowledge base. The skill areas involved include the understanding of the formal and informal functioning of politics, fund raising, the media agenda setting, networking, caucus formation and alliance building, negotiation, lobbying, leadership, and elected official, constituent relations among others. This will make more effective women's roles as voters, candidates, elected officials and political leaders, from the grassroots to the national and international levels. The training of men is also essential and can facilitate alliance building through equity caucuses and other mechanisms[5].

Since the 73rd Constitutional Amendment Act is a top down initiative, the critical mass of women are, as already discussed, facing a variety of problems. Most of the women representatives have been first timers in occupying political spaces. It is imperative that they be given opportunities for training and capacity building that informs them, strengthens and recontextualises their skills and capacities, and empowers them to become effective leaders. Given the fact that the Panchayat reforms were the product of a government fiat, the extent to which women benefited from these reforms depended upon their prior history of activism[6]. Since most of the women are new to the political space a range of factors hinder women's participation in politics including inexperience in politics and lack of exposure to it, illiteracy, family representatives and objections from family members, restrictive social norms, lack of enabling environment for women, and lack of confidence for interacting with the public. Therefore, in order to enable women's performance better in the governance, capacity building measures and support systems for women should be made available. The most dramatic criticism was that the women elected to the Village Panchayat were perceived as puppets of their male family members[7]. It is unfortunate that, in India, capacity building is not a serious issue for the representatives of the people who determine the fate of millions of people. However, in the Panchayati Raj scenario, it has been felt that, to manage the Panchayats, training is essential even though there is no training policy and no conscious steps have been taken by the government to build the capacity of the elected representatives of the people in the grassroot institutions[8].

It is also assumed that the capacity building of Elected Women Representatives will create more efficient local body leaders. It will also improve the skills and capabilities of the Elected Women Representatives. When women become more effective local government members, the Government's transparency and the delivery of resources will improve. Based on the above assumptions, the Rajiv Gandhi Chair for Panchayati Raj Studies conducted capacity building training to Elected Women Representatives in Tamil Nadu. After the elections, a series of training programmes have been organised exclusively for Gram Panchayat women leaders with the support of the Ministry of Rural Development, Government of India. In the first term (1996-2001), the Rajiv Gandhi Chair for Panchayati Raj Studies not only conducted the training programme, it also documented the problems of Elected Women Representatives. Based on its experience in capacity building exercise, it was felt that capacity and capability cannot be built into an individual overnight. It is a slow and continuous process by which the leaders can enhance their capacity practicing what they learnt in the training programme. While managing the institution and tackling the issues women leaders face a lot of problems and they are also to be tackled. It is to be taken note of that the barriers and obstacles for the women to take up power in the political process are formidable and that they require a powerful support structure beyond the training programmes to build up their skills to manage the institutions effectively and efficiently[9]. An action project was undertaken with the following objectives: (i) to build an alliance of women leaders, (ii) to conscientise them on the issues which affect the life of women, and (iii) to orient them in the methods and nuances of tackling the problems. This initiative was a demand driven one. It was taken up by the Rajiv Gandhi Chair for Panchayati Raj Studies because of the repeated requests made by the Elected Women Representatives who came to Gandhigram to attend the training programme[10].

The capacity building exercises were conducted with the training module prepared by the Rajiv Gandhi Chair for Panchayati Raj Studies. Following the preparation of the training module needed information was collected like amendments introduced on the Act, orders passed by the Government as well as rules and schemes and programmes of the Government of India and the Government of Tamil Nadu related to rural development. The Rajiv Gandhi Chair conducted residential training programmes.

The content of the programme includes basic objectives of decentralisation of powers, framework of New Panchayati Raj System, features of 73rd Constitutional Amendment Act, Tamil Nadu Panchayats Act of 1994 and its basic features, Panchayat finance and accounting, Panchayat and natural/common property resources management, people's participation in governance through Gram Sabha. Micro planning exercise, PRA/PLA approach for planning at grassroots, empowerment of weaker sections, schemes and programmes of rural development. Of the two phase training (1996-2001, 2001-2006), the second phase was scientific. In the second phase of the training programme for the EWRs, two sessions were allotted exclusively for discussing social development issues, status of women in Tamil Nadu, conditions of EWRs in Tamil Nadu, and experiences of the EWRs. Based on their experiences, EWRs are sensitised on the importance of forming networks among themselves and others.

Building Support Structure and Building Alliance

The outcome of the capacity building programme is that women leaders are demanding an institutional or organisational mechanism for the continuous flow of information and consultancy to stabilise their activities for development. The existing grassroot leader's organisations are not providing space for grievance redressal of women leaders. Moreover, the requirements of the women leaders are not adequately fulfilled by these organisations. Therefore, it has resulted in demanding a full-fledged professional organisation to assist the women local body leaders, against this background, the Rajiv Gandhi Chair for Panchayati Raj Studies decided to help with the support structure and building alliance for EWRs[11].

They established links for women representative with government agencies, NGOs, and private sector corporations. They also provided support networks and opportunities to discuss experiences, problems and issues and to plan actions to increase the accountability of both government officials and women members to their prior and other constituencies[12].

According to Yamini Narayanan, an organisation of women to experiment with forms of constructive dissent, raise questions regarding their state and society, and help them arrive at answers is a natural guarantor of development. Women also display strong group cohesion, and they show feelings of solidarity and unity, and act together, women are also most intensely involved in ensuring food security for their family.

According to India's Nobel laureate for developmental economics, Amartya Sen, an organisation of women to experiment with forms of constructive dissent, raise questions regarding their state and society, and helping them arrive at consumers is a natural guarantor of development.

After the enactment of the 73rd Constitutional Amendment Act of India, a critical mass of women entered into local bodies and capacity building to the EWRs increased their confidence to work in local bodies, but critical alliances must be sought and cemented. The Ugandan experience showed that women politicians have more impact working in teams rather than individually, and in parliamentary committees rather than in plenary[13].

Before the Rajiv Gandhi Chair helped the EWRs to network, elected local body leaders of Virudhunagar District, unlike in Thiruvarur and Ramanathapuram where Non-Governmental Organisation (NGO) facilitated Elected Women Representatives to form a network both men and women, joined together and formed a federation. When they organised a meeting with the District Collector, all went into the room of the Collector. All men leaders sat in the first three rows and the last row was given to the women leaders. There was a discussion between the leaders and the District Collector. The women leaders raised their voice, but they were asked to be silent as discussion was in progress. Finally, the men leaders said that the discussion was over and all could move out of the hall. The women leaders asked them what happened to the demands given by them. The men leaders said that those can be discussed outside the Collectors chamber. When all came out of the room, the women leaders asked them about their demands. The men leaders said that the Collector would consider them in due course. On that day the women leaders felt that the women had to adopt a different strategy and they formed a separate association. They got a separate audience with Collector and sorted out their problems. When they narrated the experience, the idea came for forming a federation. Thus, the Federation of Elected Women Representatives (exclusively women Presidents of Gram Panchayats) was born in Tamil Nadu, facilitated by the Gandhigram Rural University and other Institutions[14]. Network formation can be instigated by external or internal sources or for practical or value based reasons. Network can form either from the top down or from bottom up. A variety of network sub categories exists, including knowledge networks, sectoral networks, social change or advocacy networks, or service delivery networks. EWR networks are instigated by both internal and external sources.

Capacity building and alliance building exercise was conducted simultaneously in the I phase of the programme (1996-2001). A series of programmes were conducted to build alliances among EWRs. It started with consultation meeting on feminist perspectives in associating women representatives in local bodies.

NGOs were invited to discuss the proposed activities and the approach to be adopted for formation of network. NGOs from all-over the state participated and deliberated upon the charter of activities. They agreed upon the basic objectives of the proposal and to extend their support in carrying out the activities as partners. They divided the entire state into five zones. The activities have to be carried in all the five zones through the NGOs and NGOs have to act as nodal and zonal resource centres for the Elected Women Representatives.

Based on the NGOs consultation meetings, regional meetings were organised in five zones and problems in Panchayat administration and the problems of the women representatives were discussed.

The first regional meeting on associating women representatives in local governance was held on 21st December, 2000 at Madurai. Two coordinating agencies EKTA and RCPED in association with the other networking oragnisations from the following districts, Kanyakumari, Tirunelveli, Tuticorin, Virudhunagar, Ramanathapuram, Sivagangai, Madurai and Theni organised the programme. Elected Women Representatives of local bodies from the districts mentioned above, networking NGO representatives and the coordinating agency formed the core group. They discussed the problems faced by the women. Two women who fought against the practice of illicit liquor in Thiruvallur district were killed. They discussed abovesaid issues and they discussed the action programme and formulated it. They also discussed that all the government orders are not reaching to the Panchayat Presidents. So far 98 Panchayat Presidents in Tamil Nadu are removed from their position by using section 205 of the Tamil Nadu Panchayat Act. Out of 98, 66 are women out of 66 women representatives, 44 have proved that they have not committed any mistake in administration and as a result all of them got reinstated in their position. When they are in trouble, they need support base. They discussed and formed, "Tamil Nadu Southern District Panchayat Women Representatives Federation". Office bearers were elected for the federation.

With the help of Sevalaya (a non-governmental organisation) facilitation, Rajiv Gandhi Chair for Panchayati Raj Studies organised meeting for the Elected Women Representatives of Thiruvarur and Nagapattinam Districts. The Elected Women Representatives already have been enlightened on the importance of network due to the non-governmental organisations facilitation. They moved further the type of network that they have to form. Accordingly they formed Tamil Nadu Thiruvarur, Nagapattinam District Panchayat Women Representatives Federation. Sevalaya agreed to provide office space.

The meeting for the Elected Women Representatives belong to northern districts namely Villupuram, Thiruvannamalai, Tiruvallur, Kancheepuram, Vellore, Cuddalore was held on 16th February 2001 with the assistance of LRSA, Chengalpet. Dalit women leaders of abovesaid districts participated. In the meeting, the Elected Women Representatives decided that a district level association exclusively for Dalit Presidents must be made at each district and consultation and discussion must be organised to strengthen the functioning of the association. The network/association must be registered body under the Societies Registration Act. Finally, Villupuram, Kancheepuram district alone formed the association.

The central regions comprising of ten districts is known for active women organisation NGOs and political parties. A few of these districts are highly industrialised and few other are known for their agricultural prosperity. The concept of Self-Help Group is found to be its peak in few districts. The fourth regional workshop meeting for the districts namely Karur, Namakkal, Erode, Salem, Trichy, Perambalur, Pudukkottai, Nilgiris and Coimbatore was held on 21st March, 2001. They discussed problems pertaining to common property resource management. They formed district level network with NGO as a member of the network.

After the zonal meeting, an Annual Convention was held in Gandhigram. EWRs from all-over the state of Tamil Nadu participated in the meeting. Apart from the EWRs, women activists, NGO representatives, media persons were invited to participate in the meeting. EWRs shared their experience. Problems of the EWRs and the experience of the EWRs were documented for policy advocacy.

Further the EWRs decided to visit model Panchayats in other states. The interface to visit Kerala Panchayats was arranged by Rajiv Gandhi Chair for Panchayati Raj Studies for 100 Elected Women Representatives.

After the election in Tamil Nadu, in the month of October 2001, training modules were prepared to conduct the training programme for EWRs. EWRs who were elected for the second term participated in the programme. During January 2002, from 20th to 24th, a networking meeting and an interface programme were organised. In the network meeting, the Elected Women Representatives took up some key issues for discussion and these were sent to the Director of Rural Development. In the interface meeting, the Elected Women Representatives interacted with their counterparts from Kerala[15]. The Elected Women Representatives Federation has been trying to get the Central Minister to attend their meeting for discussion. Mr. Venkaiah Naidu, the Minister for Rural Development, Government of India, participated in EWRs meeting on 20th February, 2002.

The Second Annual Meeting was conducted on 3rd May, 2002. Academicians, IAS officials, representatives of the media participated.

EWRs discussed the 15-point programme of the Government of Tamil Nadu.

After the two years of network activities, the following suggestions were made:

1. Deepen the federation.
2. Encourage federation at lower level.
3. Partnership with press has to be created.
4. Using the government order issued earlier periodical meetings have to be organised at the district level.
5. For official intervention at local levels, district level leaders have to be contacted.
6. To contact the officials at state level, state level official have to be contacted.
7. While meeting the convention, the issues of women have to be discussed.

In the second phase capacity building was conducted for the EWRs of 13 districts. During the training programme, district level federations were formed. Office bearers were elected both at district level and block level. There are about 450 EWRs federated.

Elected Women Representatives conducted special meeting on 9th May, 2002 to analyse and evaluate critically the possible role the Panchayats could play in the process of implementation of the 15-point programme.

Apart from the above they conducted executive committee in Gandhigram on 2nd December to analyse the current problems faced by the Elected Women Representatives.

They regularly meet state level officials, and they met on 28th January, 2003 and submitted problems, the Gram Panchayats are facing. They requested Director of Rural Development, Government of Tamil Nadu to take immediate action.

Apart from the above meetings, interface with officials, interfaces with media, interface with representatives were conducted to build a support structure for EWRs. Creation of an interface means formatting routine interaction among key stakeholders and delivering services in rural communities. Their relationship and interdependence from the training of elements essential to good governance is seen in Fig. 4.1.

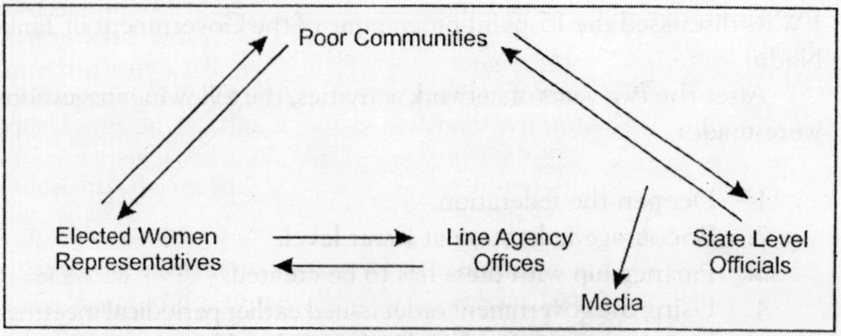

Fig. 4.1: Relationship and Interdependence.

Stakeholder in a complex social environment provided with training, assets, or resources, the results are often not effective. For example, line officers have often wanted to deliver services more effectively, but reaching their target populations may be hampered because locally elected officials responsible for providing accurate recipient lists are not involved. Moreover, the groups targeted for assistance are often unaware of resources designated for them, miss out on benefits to which they are entitled and can't act as pressure groups to hold government officials and locally elected members accountable. When key stakeholders have access to information, the capacity to understand and deliver resources, and the ability to monitor and facilitate pro-poor activities, local government is likely to improve, and poor constituents are more likely to be included in programmes designed for them. Through the interface, women members were able to work with government properly and social sector programmes[16].

It is assumed that training and awareness could bring women representatives to a better position not only in participation level but also in decision-making. The assistance given by the NGOs through the various training programmes and general awareness programmes is worth noting. The need for training of women does not mean that women were incapable of undertaking development at local level perceived by men politicians but for qualitative input in development works taken up by the government, which did not reach those who actually needed it. Training has been identified as an important tool to carry out development activities. Training is essential especially for women because their participation in local government and in the public sphere is a new phenomenon. The capacity building exercise and networking build a vision among EWRs on:

- Forming Self-Help Groups and utilising their service.
- Creating awareness about personal hygiene among women.
- Constructing toilets in balwadis, schools and every house.
- Providing drinking water supply.
- Making Panchayats as a model one.
- Making Panchayats Hut free.
- Construction of Primary Health Centers.
- Installation of rainwater harvesting structure.
- Abolition of plastics.

The capacity building exercise and regular association meetings helped women Panchayat leaders to concentrate on social development issues like retrieving common property resource management, ensuring entitlements of poor through Public Distribution System and getting reservation for women for ten years. In the federation meetings women leaders discussed day to day activities of Panchayats as well as social issues and solutions and suggestions were provided. The women leaders are keen to internalise the issues.

Summary

The abovesaid experience has emerged from the grassroots. This was facilitated by the individuals and institutions. Few political parties and leaders also realised the potentials of the association and they regularly interacted with them. The president of EWR association of Tamil Nadu has a link with the Association of Local Government in India (ALGI, New Delhi) and she is the state organiser of Tamil Nadu for ALGI. The federation has also become a registered institution with the broader vision and objectives of working with all those who come forward to extend their support to the process of women empowerment. According to the above case study it may be inferred that the network helped many EWRs to sort out their problems. The regular participation of network meeting provided awareness on social development issues, interaction with feminist and gender experts, concientised EWRs on gender issues. Capacity building exercise helped them to inculcate leadership qualities. Finally, the network facilitated members to create and disseminate best practices, improved interventions and approaches, strengthened participation, collaboration and created new ways of learning working together. After the 2006 election few women leaders got re-elected due to the changing rotation pattern and also women's organisations and movements are trying to own and impose their ideologies on association instead of recognising and strengthening the association for the development of the governance at the grassroots. The challenges for the future are— the ideological differences among network members, diverse social background and different agendas. This may result in the formation of different small networks. Integrating the small network and making them to form a broader network is the greatest challenge. Lack of vision for the future and the lack of fund also pose the challenge for the sustainability of the network. The challenge is to keep the network and make them work as a collective group and strengthening the network at the block level.

NOTES

1. G. Palanithurai, *Empowerment of Women: Problems Faced by the Elected Women Representatives in Tamil Nadu*, Gandhigram: Rajiv Gandhi Chair for Panchayati Raj Studies, 2001.
2. G. Palanithurai and V. Ragupathy, *Building Alliances and Capabilities among the Elected Women Representatives of Grassroots Institutions*, Gandhigram: Rajiv Gandhi Chair for Panchayati Raj Studies, 2003.
3. S. Wieringa, "Women's Interests and Empowerment: Gender Planning Recognised", *Development and Change*, 25, 1994.
4. UNDP, *Human Development Report 1995: Gender and Development*, Oxford: Oxford University Press, 1995.
5. UNDP, *Women's Political Participation: 21st Century Challenges*, New Delhi: UNDP, 2000.
6. Amrita Basu, "Gender and Governance: Concepts and Contexts", in *UNDP: Essays on Gender and Governance*, New Delhi: UNDP: 2003.
7. Lina Hamaden Banarjee, "Think Globally, Elect Locally? in UNDP: *Women's Political Participation and Good Governance: 21st Century Challenges*, New Delhi: UNDP, 2000.
8. G. Palanithurai, *Capacity Building Grassroots Leaders, to Panchayati Raj Studies*, Gandhigram: Rajiv Gandhi Chair for Panchayati Raj Studies, 2004.
9. G. Palanithurai, V. Ragupathy, *Building Alliances and Capabilities among*

the Elected Women Representatives of Grassroots Institutions, Gandhigram: Rajiv Gandhi Chair for Panchayati Raj Studies, 2003

10. *Ibid.*
11. Rajiv Gandhi Chair for Panchayati Raj Studies, *Report of the state level consultation on feminist perspectives in associating women representatives in associating women leadership*, Gandhigram: Rajiv Gandhi Chair for Panchayati Raj Studies, 2000.
12. Asian Development Bank, *Gender and Governance issues in Local Government, Regional Report of Technical Assistance in Bangladesh, Nepal, and Pakistan*, Manila: Asian Development Bank, 2004.
13. Lina Hamaden, Banarjee, "Think Globally, Elect Locally" in *Women's Political Participation and Good Governance: 21st Century Challenges*, New Delhi: UNDP, 2000.
14. G. Palanithurai (Ed.), *Are They Withdrawing from Public Space?* Gandhigram: Rajiv Gandhi Chair for Panchayati Raj Studies, 2005.
15. Rajiv Gandhi Chair for Panchayati Raj Studies, *Report on State Level NGOs Network Meet in Associating Women Representatives in Local Bodies*, Gandhigram: Rajiv Gandhi Chair for Panchayati Raj Studies, 2000.
16. Isharat Bhamin, Ranhana Kumari, *Gender and Local Governance: A New Discourse in Development*, Report submitted to South Asia Network of Economic Research Institutes, submitted by Centre for Women and Children Studies, Dhaka Bangladesh and Centre for Social Research, New Delhi, India, Nov., 2002.

5

Federating Elected Women Representatives in Tamil Nadu

G. PALANITHURAI

Introduction

The 73rd Amendment to the Constitution of India has created a legitimate space for women in governance and development by reserving seats in all the tiers of rural local governance for women not less than one-third of the strength of the total population in every unit of rural local governance. It has given a sense that the critical mass has been created at every level and thereby one can expect a critical function at every level by the effective, efficient and total involvement of the critical mass formed through reservation of seats for women. When they involve themselves in critical function, critical issues of development will be addressed and there a society will witness transformation of the society[1]. With the above assumption questions have been asked about the impact created by the elected women representatives in the rural society and more specifically among the rustic folk. As an academic activist I know that women in South Asia can be looked at from the perspective of West. Women in South Asia are in different socio-economic and cultural settings[2]. Further the critical mass theory which had been evolved in the West based on their experience cannot be applied here as the critical mass formed in

India is really not a critical mass in substance and strength but it is only numbers. But the numbers can be transformed into really a critical mass. How to do it? is a major question. Rajiv Gandhi Chair for Panchayati Raj Studies had been created in 1996 in Gandhigram Rural Institute with an objective of strengthening local governance system in India by building up a movement at grassroots through various strategies and of which building capacity, Skill, Capability of the elected women representatives is one and important[3]. Hence, we have involved in capacity building activities for elected women representatives in Tamil Nadu with the support of CAPART and the Hunger Project[4].

Training modules have been evolved and manual has been prepared and capacity building capacity exercise had been carried out[5]. But the problem came only after the elected representatives went to the field with a new vision, commitment and energy after the training. They have faced volley of problems in the field[6]. Having said in the training programme that Rajiv Gandhi Chair is not only an organisation to conduct training programme but it will continue to facilitate elected women representatives to perform their responsibilities effectively and efficiently. When the elected women representatives came for hand hold support what the chair can do was a daunting question before us. At that point of time the new idea of federating elected women representatives came and it was made into a reality through a project supported by the Ford Foundation. Though we took initiative we have decided deliberately that the organisation or Federation in whatever form the elected women representatives develop that should be facilitated by Rajiv Gandhi Chair. But proper perspective has to be developed for the federation activities.

Developing an Approach

With this objective, reputed action oriented feminists, gender specialists, lawyers, representatives from NGOs and academics were invited to deliberate upon the strategies and the approaches to be adopted for a transformation process through the women's organisation. The elected women representatives were invited to share their experience with the feminists and gender specialists. On 26th

August, 2000, they deliberated upon the prevailing environment in the rural society for the functioning of the local bodies under the leadership of the women drawn from different socio-economic conditions.

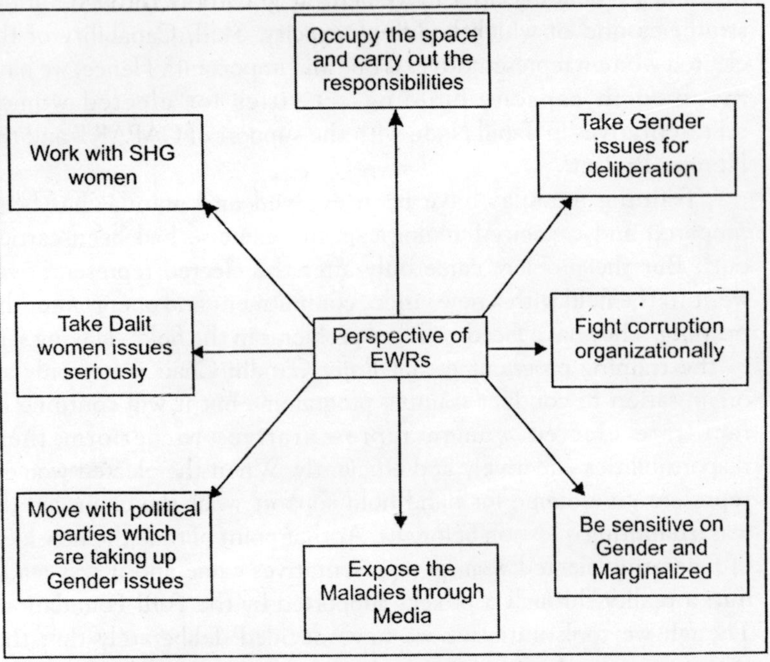

Fig. 5.1: Perspective Building for EWRs.

In this consultation exercise, the following actions and approaches were evolved[7]. As a first step, the loosely organised associations have to be federated into a cohesive movement to address the issues of the women and the marginalised. To do this, regional meetings have to be organised and zonal or regional units have to be created for furthering the activities of the federation. While organising such regional meetings, the problems faced by the women leaders have to be properly documented for policy advocacy and they have to be published through media. Leaders from different regions are to be gathered for periodical meetings and they have to be sensitised on the basic issues of development like food security, livelihood security and more specifically on the issues of women. While sensitising the women these issues are to be discussed contextually futuristically. To gain confidence, they need hands on experience for which meaningful interface programmes could be organised on demand by taking these leaders from Tamil Nadu to Kerala and even from one region to another region within Tamil Nadu where success cases are reported.

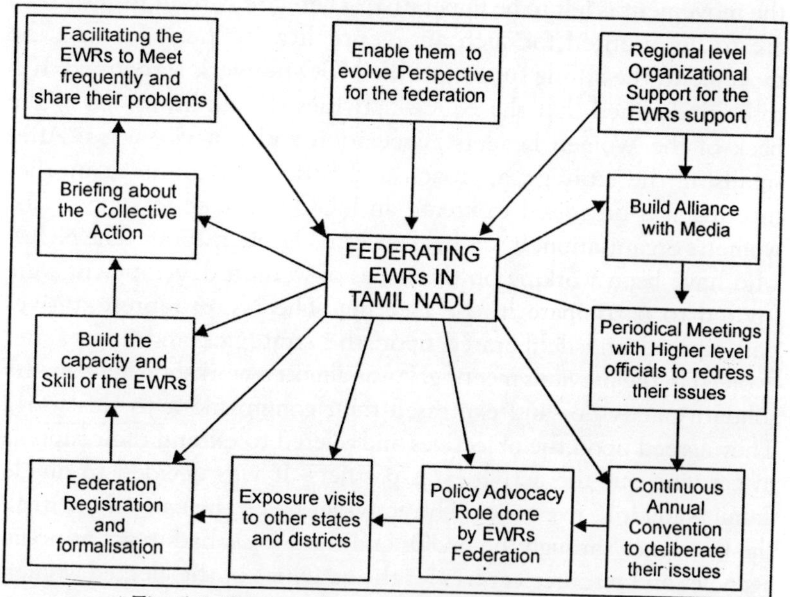

Fig. 5.2: Envisaged Activities for EWRs Federation.

An annual Elected Women Leaders convention has to be organised where the documented problems of different regions have to be discussed in front of dignarities and the media for popular dissemination and corrective action. The discussed issues have to be taken to the policy making level for lobbying for which Gandhigram Rural Institute should take up the responsibility. Through the regional outfits, needed information has to be provided periodically to the Panchayat leaders. The elected women representatives who are struggling in the Panchayat administration to deliver services should be given helping hand by which it can be demonstrated to the other leader's hat behind them and very many civil society organisations.

To develop this movement the elected women representatives have to be trained in Panchayat management. They should be provided with needed skills and capability. Further the leaders of the Association in different regions are to be oriented in providing leadership to the other elected women representatives. To add visibility to the issues of women and their organization, a proper sensitization is necessary for women in governance and the issue of women. The media's role in the movement is felt to be imperative. There are certain issues which are to be oriented for such an eventuality. To push forward the movement, the strong support of the NGO network is required. It is to be underlined that the NGOs activities should always be at the back of the Women Leaders Association and not *vice versa*. After finalising the strategy, approach and action programme, another meeting was organised to create an NGO network to support the women's organisation. It was held on 23rd October, 2000[8]. The NGOs who have been working on the issues of women development were invited to participate in the meeting. The NGO representatives participated and deliberated upon the strategies and approaches evolved in the previous meeting. It was almost a workshop for women's solidarity activities and expressed their commitment to this work. They agreed upon the objectives and offered to extend their support in carrying out the activities as partners. It was decided to divide Tamil Nadu into five zones. The activities had to be carried out in all the five zones through the NGOs and the NGOs had to act as nodal agencies and resource centres for the activities of the elected women representatives.

Following this commitment of the NGOs, regional meetings were organised at Madurai on 21st December, 2000 at Thiruvarur on 2nd February, 2001, at Chengalpattu on 16th February, 2001, and at Karur on 21st March, 2001[9]. In all regional or zonal meetings, the problems faced by the elected women representatives in administering development were discussed and documented. The documents were published and circulated among the representatives of the media for wider dissemination. The problems had to be taken to different levels for redressal. So they were classified and they were taken to the Block Development Office and to the State Legislative Assembly for redressal. On 5th August, 2001, an annual conversion of the women leaders was organised at Gandhigram and it discussed the basic issues of the women, strategies to overcome the problems and the problems faced by the panchayats[10]. As they discussed the issues thoroughly all the issues were fully covered in the media which brought visibility to the women's federation.

Interface Meetings

After the Zonal or regional meetings and the annual convention, it was decided to undertake the interface programme under which the federation leaders were taken to Kerala to visit some of the panchayats and held discussion with the leaders and functionaries on the issues of development. They concentrated more on the issues of social and economic development almost all the federation leaders got an opportunity to visit Kerala to have a glimpse of the social and economic development activities of the Gram Panchayats[11].

The elected women representatives tried to bring the Minister for Rural Development, Government of India, to their programme and succeeded in their attempt. On 20th February, 2002, Mr.Venkaiah Naidu participated in their programme wherein the elected representatives discussed their issues with him and appealed to him to intervene at the appropriate level to redress their grievance. Along with the Minister, State level officials also participated and they were all asked by the Rural Development Minister to give replies to the questions raised by the representatives[12].

They organised the Second Annual Meet in Gandhigram on 3rd May, 2002. In the second annual meeting, they discussed the 15-point programme of the Government of Tamil Nadu. In the course of the discussion they pointed out that, out of the 15-points, about 13 come under the purview of the Panchayati Raj Institutions. They went on to clarify at what level they can work and to what extent officials have to work to achieve the target. They compiled guidelines by which the details of the earmarked responsibilities could be identified[13]. For the annual meet they invited the Director of Rural Development, Government of Tamil Nadu, Mr. S. Ayyar, I.A.S. They made a powerful plea that in each and every district the District Collector has to convene a meeting of Gram Panchayat women leader and redress their problems in the management of the Panchayats. He agreed to do so and promised to issue an order in this regard[14]. They further decided to form an advisory council consisting of retired officials, representatives from NGOs, academics and representatives from the media to facilitate the functioning of the federation. Subsequently, based on the deliberations of the Second Annual Convention, a regional leader's meet was organised on 9th May, 2002 to make an in-depth study of the 15-point programme and the problems faced by the women leaders[15] and consolidate their demands to be presented to the Government of Tamil Nadu.

Implications

So far the sequence of events has been presented. But the implications of the activities have to be explained. One should not assume that the federation met once a year and deliberated only in Gandhigram. They organised several meetings in several places with the help of other NGOs also. They met political party leaders and officials for presenting their charter of demands. They used to meet the press periodically and express their opinion on vital issues which affect the life of the people, particularly women, children and dalits[16]. Based on the training programme, we have collected the problems faced by the Panchayati leaders generally, and women and dalit leaders specifically, and those problems have been documented by our centre. These documents have been used by this federation for policy advocacy. It was very difficult for them to get information regarding Government Orders, rules and schemes. But now they are being received from Gandhigram Rural Institute and so they regard it as a resource centre. Contacting Ministers, higher officials, MPs and MLAs is no more a problem for them. Women leaders who are in this federating arrangement are highly sensitised on the issues of social development and more specifically on the issues of women and children. When state government's proposal to introduce cheap liquor came as the most unkindest cut of all for the women heading village panchayats, the women presidents reacted sharply that they were let down by a woman Chief Minister. They unequivocally argued and made it clear that they would launch an agitation if the Government refused to drop the proposal. When the regional leaders of the Federation met at Gandhigram, they discussed this issue at length and spoke to the Hindu Special Reporter Mr. S.Annamalai that they have been fighting at the village level for the past five years to eradicate illicit liquor, but now the Government itself seeks to introduce liquor to make money. Subsequently, the move was withdrawn in the rural areas. It was considered a victory for the women Panchayat leader's Federation.

Subsequently, in 2002, in the month of December, when they met at Gandhigram, they made a plea to the Government of Tamil Nadu to increase the revenue of the Panchayats. The women Panchayat leader's Federation suggested that the State Government can hand over the common properties to the Panchayats. They indicated that quarries, tanks and trees which now under the control of the Government's agencies and individuals would fetch adequate revenue to make the local bodies self-reliant. They projected an alternative model of resource mobilisation for Panchayats.

As they attend periodical meetings of the Federation, the restrictions imposed on them have been gradually removed. Without the assistance of the males of their family they travel to Chennai, Madurai and Trichy to attend the meetings of the federation. Further their communicative ability has improved to a surprising level as the grassroots women leaders have developed their own style of communication which has been accepted as a formal mode of communication. Their bargaining capability has been enhanced to strike a deal with officials, MLAs and MPs for the benefit of the people. The feeling of isolation that prevailed among the elected women representatives has gone as they meet frequently and share their joys and difficulties. When the elected women representatives face problems in administration, the Federation leaders take the issue to the District Collector and to the level of the Director for Rural Development. They get their problems redressed, failing which they go to court and get suitable legal remedy which has raised the morale of the women leaders. Frequent sharing has built up the idea that this kind of exercise is necessary for their success. Their media contact is frequent and its implications are also positive.

Though Tamil Nadu has a District Panchayat Presidents Association, a Block Panchayat Association, and a Gram Panchayat Association, only the Federation of Women Panchayat Leaders Association is visible and reacts sharply on many of the vital issues. Even though the elected women representatives have a charter of demands, they are keener on getting reservation of seats for women for ten years, retrieving common properties from encroachment, and ensuring the entitlements of the poor through the public distribution system. Active leaders in the Federation are very much sensitised on these social development issues after visiting the Kerala Panchayats. During the first period the women leaders were harping on transfer of power, finance and functionaries. Now they speak about issues and problems. They have gained voice and bargaining power.

One major achievement that they have scored through their work is getting the reservation of seats for women in local bodies extended for one more term. It is unique in the whole of the country. Another important achievement is that the Federation has made the State Government withdraw the plan for cheap liquor. They pleaded with the Government that every month higher level officials at the district level should convene such meetings and solve the problems of the women leaders.

Because of their repeated pleas and activities, the Federation of Women Leaders Association is visible to the policy makers and 33.3 per cent of seats have been reserved for women even in co-operative societies also. Likewise an order has been issued that in all statutory committees one-third reservations should be provided for women. Some of the women panchayat leaders were in deep trouble. It was only the Federation which saved them. Menaka, the President of Oorappakam, was murdered in the panchayat office due her stern action against enrichment. No FIR was filed till the Federation leaders went to the Panchayat. It was only because of this federation that the culprits were booked. Another interesting noteworthy feature is that more number of office bearers in the Federation is now from the Dalit community and the Federation has focused its attention on dalit issues (Fig. 5.3).

Learnings

Elected women leaders are of different categories. They are educated, uneducated, highly sophisticated, rich, poor, wage earners, dalits and others. They are leaders with political orientation and party background. They look at the issues only from their party perspective. There are leaders who have commitments and values but no awareness and information. There are leaders with high political aspirations. It is to be noted that the leaders who are deeply committed to the issues

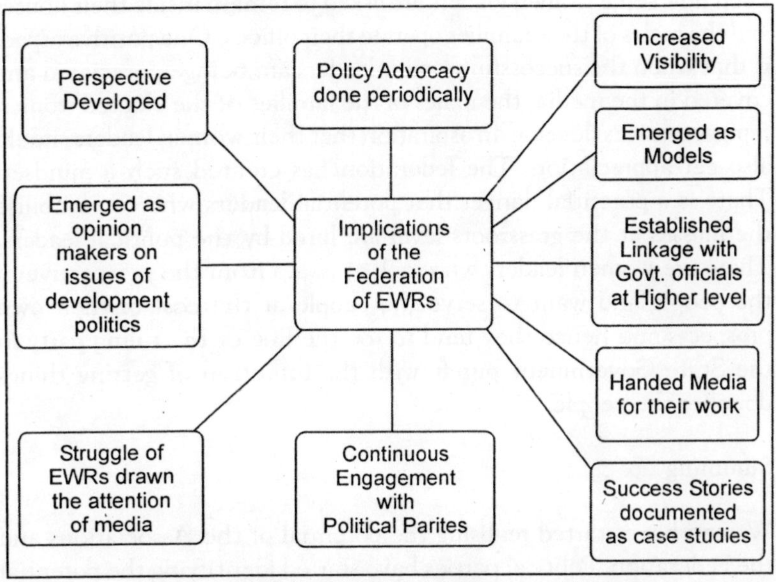

Fig. 5.3: Implications of the Federation of EWRs.

of the people without political background continue to be active members of Federation. The Federation attracts more number of Gram Panchayat women leaders as the Gram Panchayat is freed from the party fold and the problems focused on in the Federation are mostly the problems faced by the Gram Panchayat women leaders. One layer of elected women representatives is alert and they are oriented and conscientised but the other segments are not so well oriented. When oriented and motivated leaders take up the development issues, they face a volley of problems. To tackle all these problems they require support structure. They demand periodical sensitisation on vital issues affecting women and other marginalised groups. They require periodical update on Government orders and new schemes of the government. They are in need of periodical interface programmes. The federation of elected women representatives does not include all the women leaders of rural and urban local bodies. Those who have come out despite obstacles and barriers and those who are struggling with determination have joined together. A large number of elected representatives have not come out of their houses and have not even visited their offices. The federation is slowly moving towards them.

Even now some women leaders are asked to remain inside their houses and the males of their families operate their offices. One positive aspect is that when the successful women leaders are being appreciated and covered in the media, the males of the families of the elected women representatives develop an aspiration that their women leaders should also get appreciation. The federation has created such a mindset. There is a potential danger that potential leaders who can mobilise the masses at the grassroots level are lured by the political leaders. There are women leaders who look at issues from the perspective of the people and want to serve the people at the cost of their own prospects and hence they tend to toe the line of the ruling party in the State Government purely with the intention of getting things done for the people.

Summing up

Women have started realising the potential of the Associations and the Federation. Political parties have started identifying the potential leaders from Gram Panchyats and enlisting them as their party members and proclaiming their achievements as the achievements of the party. The media has been sensitised on the woman issues and as a result the media has given wide coverage to the activities of the women's federation. Elected women representatives have learnt the art of managing bureaucracy. They have picked up communication skills. They have developed bargaining power. Moving with higher officials has become a routine affair and the fear to meet the District Collector and other higher officials has gone. A large number of new leaders are drawn from self group towards the panchayats. Sharing the struggles and achievements in the regional and annual conventions has motivated other women leaders to emulate them. The fear syndrome and the dependency syndrome have gone. The group activities have developed a positive attitude among the women leaders to strive for achievements.

The following constitute the 15-point Programme of the Government of Tamil Nadu.

Rajiv Gandhi Chair, **Role of Local Bodies in the Process of Implementation of 15-Point Programme,** Gandhigram: Rajiv Gandhi Chair, 2002

The Honourable Chief Minister, Selvi. J.Jayalalitha, has announced her commitment to make Tamil Nadu the best state in the country in every sphere. "To provide opportunities for a healthy and productive life for all" will be the goal of this Government. This vision will be realised through the implementation of the Chief Minister's 15-points programme which will encompass the following:

i. ***Evergreen revolution***: Raising farm Productivity in Perpetuity: Saving every drop of rain: More crop per drop.
ii. Food security: Physical, economic and social access to balanced diets to every child, woman and man.
iii. ***Livestock Security***: Upgradation of livestock, better veterinary care: supplementing farm income: improving fish diversity and increasing fish density.
iv. ***Water Security***: Safe drinking water and adequate water for agriculture, industry and ecosystem maintenance.
v. ***Health Security***: Control of all diseases including leprosy, tuberculosis, preventable blindness, and eradication of diseases for which effective vaccines are available: reduction in birth and death rates increases in average life span: Reduction of Infant Mortality (IMR), Maternal Mortality Rate (MMR) and incidence of low birth weight children: adoption of a maternal and child care code; fight against HIV/AIDS; special attention to physically and mentally handicapped children, women and men.
vi. ***Livelihood Security***: "Work for All" and transition from unskilled to skilled work; integrated attention to rural on-farm and non-farm employment as well as to micro-enterprises supported by micro-credit; A New Deal to the self-employed through technology, training, techno-infrastructure and domestic and external trade.
vii. ***Shelter Security***: Promotion of housing activities designed to harvest sun and rain so that solar energy capture and rainwater harvesting become everybody's business.

viii. ***Ecological Security***: Conservation and enhancement of life support system like land, water, forest, bio-diversity, Ocean and the atmosphere; Recycling of solid and liquid wastes and composting of all organic wastes; Safe disposal of hospital wastes; Bio-environmental control of malaria.

ix. ***Energy Security***: Building sustainable energy systems with concurrent attention to thermal, hydro, nuclear and renewable forms of energy like wind, solar, biogas and biomass; energy self-sufficiency for the farm, industrial and domestic sectors.

x. ***Infrastructure for Development***: Provision of basic amenities in rural and urban areas; Connectivity to all habitation with population above 500; bridging the rural-urban divide.

xi. ***Literacy and Technicacy***: Attention to quality improvement in education ranging from the pre-school to university; Special attention to the technological and skill empowerment of illiterate or semi-literate women and men; eradication of child labour.

xii. ***Folk, classical and modern arts, culture and drama***: Generation of awareness and appreciation of the cultural heritage of Tamil Nadu and revitalisation of cultural traditions, including the street theatre.

xiii. ***Gender Equity***: Removal of gender bias, elimination of adverse sex ratio, and support services to working women, taking into account the multiple burdens on a woman's day-to-day life.

xiv. ***New Deal for the Oppressed Classes***: Educational and economic empowerment of the Adi-Dravidas, Scheduled Tribes, backward classes, most backward classes, and denotified tribes.

xv. ***Technological Leapfrogging***: Promotion of research and development in frontier areas of sciences and technology like biotechnology and information technology, coordination of efforts between academic know-how and field level do how. Launching a movement for fostering greater public understanding of sciences and promoting a new social contact between scientists and society; providing equal attention to connectivity and content in efforts to bridge the digital divide; including access to appropriate technologies in the basic minimum needs programme.

The Chief Minister's 15-points programme outlined here will be the road map for this Government in the next four years. It will be the endeavour of this Government to realise this vision by March 2006.

Their activities are covered in the press. The details are:

New Indian Express 06.05.2002	Panchayat chiefs favour Govt. Programmes. Women leaders keen on development activities of Panchayats.
Dinamalar 12.01.2002	Nanillam Union—Panchayat Leaders meet
Dinamani 13.01.2002	Network meeting of SSF – Thiruvarur Cheap Liquor Scheme/Hitting below the belt
Dinamalar 10.05.2002	Second Annual Meet of SSF Director of Rural Development – suggest
Dinamani 29.04.2002	Annual Conference of Women Leaders at State Level
Dina Thanthi 01.05.2002	Annual Conference of Women Leaders at State Level
The Hindu 02.05.2002	Elected Women Representatives Meet
Dina Thanthi 04.05.2002	Elected Women Representatives Meet
The Hindu 04.05.2002	Information Kiosks coming up for SHGs in 10 Districts
The Hindu 08.12.2001	Cheap Liquor scheme/Hitting below the belt Women feel let down by a women
Theekkathir 21.12.2001	Funds to local bodies plan to file PIL
Dinamalar 05.03.2002	A Modified Family Card – Leader did – Minister encouraged
Dina Thanthi 04.12.2001	Satisfying the basic needs – Funds to local bodies – A request
The Financial Express 19.12.2001	Tamil Nadu Panchayats plan to file PIL for release of Statutory Grants
News Today 20.12.2001	Funds to local bodies 'relent or face a stir' women Panchayat chiefs on warpath
Dinamani 20.12.2001	Funds to local bodies 'relent or face a stir' women Panchayat chiefs on warpath
Dina Thanthi 20.12.2001	Funds to local bodies 'relent or face a stir' women Panchayat chiefs on warpath
Dinamalar 20.12.2001	Allot 20 per cent of MLA and MP fund to Panchayats—Leaders wish
Dinakaran 20.12.2001	EWRs meet at Chennai a crisis on implementing activities struggle on cheap liquor scheme
The Hindu 03.04.2002	No nomination for wards, Polls went Empower Dalits
The Hindu 19.03.2002	Spell out Stand on Devolution: Tamil Nadu Panchayat
Dinamani 06.11.2001	Fulfill the responsibilities and commit your needy Dr. Pankajam, Vice-Chancellor, GRI – suggest
The Hindu 08.11.2001	Village Panchayats told to concentrate on tax collection

New Indian express 22.02.2002	Centre fixes target of 14 lakh SHG—M.Venkaiah Naidu, Rural Development Minister, Govt. of India at GRI.
The Hindu 16.02.2002	Participatory development key to Panchayat Raj
Dinamalar 16.02.2002	From education to family planning – need for a change in training the leaders
Dinamani 15.02.2002	New method of training to the president – suggest
The Hindu 13.01.2001	Panchayat chiefs play key role in primary education
Dinamani 12.01.2002	Panchayat chiefs play key role in primary education
The Hindu 20.12.2001	Women Panchayat chiefs threaten stir
New Indian Express 18.12.2001	Bureaucrats treat women Panchayat president as servants
Dina Thanthi 07.10.2001	Women Panchayat chiefs threaten stir. Say 'No' to corruption in Panchayat
The Hindu 06.10.2001	Women Panchayat chiefs threaten stir. Say 'No' to corruption in Panchayat
Dinakaran 06.10.2001	Women Panchayat chiefs threaten stir. Say 'No' to corruption in Panchayat

NOTES

1. Drade Dahberup, "From a Small to a Large Minority: Women in Scandinavian Politics" ,*Scandinavian Political Studies* 1988, Vol 11: No 4, pp. 275-298; M.Bystdzienski Jill; *Women Transforming Politics: Worldwide Strategies for Empowerment*. Iniana Pobis: Indiana University Press, 1992.
2. Damyanty Sridharan and Rodic Vesna (eds), *Breaking the Political Glass Ceiling: Women and Local Governance in South Asia*, New Delhi: Freidrich Ebert Stifftung, 2004.
3. G.Palanithurai, "The Empowerment Process: Women Representatives in Grassroots Institutions in Tamil Nadu", *Indian Social Science Review*, vol 6: No. 2, Jan-June, 2004.
4. G.Palanithurai, *Capacity Building for Local Body Leaders*, New Delhi: Concept Publishing Company, 2003.
5. G.Palanithurai, *Training Modules for Leadership*, Gandhigram: Rajiv Gandhi Chair for Panchayati Raj Studies, 1998.
6. G.Palanithurai, *Empowerment of Women: Experiences of the Women Representatives in Grassroots Institutions*, Gandhigram: Rajiv Gandhi Panchayati Raj Studies, 2002.
7. Detailed proceedings are reported in the document. For more details, see Rajiv Gandhi Chair, *State Level Consultation on Feminist Perspective*

in Associating Women Representatives in Local Bodies: A Report, Gandhigram: Rajiv Gandhi Chair for Panchayati Raj Studies, 2000.

8. For more details about the discussion, see Rajiv Gandhi Chair, *A Report on State Level NGO's Network meet on Associating Women Representatives in local bodies*, Gandhigram, Rajiv Gandhi Chair for Panchayati Raj Studies, 2000.
9. The entire discussions and deliberations have been documented. For more details refer to the following documents: Rajiv Gandhi Chair, *A Report on Regional Level Meets on Associating Women Representatives in Local Bodies– I*, Gandhigram: Rajiv Gandhi Chair for Panchayati Raj Studies, 2000.
   Rajiv Gandhi Chair, *A Report on Regional Level Meet on Associating Women Representatives in Local Bodies*–II, Gandhigram: Rajiv Gandhi Chair for Panchayati Raj Studies, 2001.
   Rajiv Gandhi Chair, *A Report on Regional Level Meet on Associating Women Representatives in Local Bodies*–III, Gandhigram: Rajiv Gandhi Chair for Panchayati Raj Studies, 2001.
   Rajiv Gandhi Chair, *A Report on Regional Level Meet on Associating Women Representatives in Local Bodies*–IV, Gandhigram: Rajiv Gandhi Chair for Panchayati Raj Studies, 2001.
10. Rajiv Gandhi Chair, *The Annual Convention of the Elected Women Representatives in Tamil Nadu: A Report*, Gandhigram: Rajiv Gandhi Chair for Panchayati Raj Studies, 2001.
11. Rajiv Gandhi Chair, *A Report on First Networking Meeting and Interface Programme*, Gandhigram: Rajiv Gandhi Chair for Panchayati Raj Studies, 2002.
12. Rajiv Gandhi Chair, *A Report on Second Networking Meeting and Interface Programme*, Gandhigram: Rajiv Gandhi Chair for Panchayati Raj Studies, 2002.
13. Rajiv Gandhi Chair, *A Report on Women Panchayat Leaders Meet on 20-02-2002*, Gandhigram: Rajiv Gandhi Chair for Panchayati Raj Studies, 2002.
14. Rajiv Gandhi Chair, *Report of the Second Annual Meet of Elected Women Representatives*, Gandhigram, Rajiv Gandhi Chair for Panchayati Raj Studies, 2001.
15. Letter received from the Director Rural Development, Government of Tamil Nadu dated 20-05-2002.
16. Rajiv Gandhi Chair, *Report of the Special Meet of the Elected Women Representatives of Local Bodies at Gandhigram*, Gandhigram: Rajiv Gandhi Chair for Panchayati Raj Studies, 2002.

6

Report of the National Workshop

Synthesis of a National Workshop: Strengthening Women's Leadership in Local Governments through Collectives and Federations

7th to 9th September 2010, Hotel Clarion, New Delhi

Local Governance Inititative South Asia (LoGln),
a Project of SDC, India

Background

Since the late 90s right up to 2009, Swiss Agency for Development and Cooperation (SDC) in India has been supporting programmes of the state and civil society aimed at strengthening local governance and decentralisation. Presently, SDC is implementing a project, 'Local Governance Initiative (LoGIn) South Asia' which is aimed at promoting south-south and north-south knowledge exchange on decentralisation and local governance. In India LoGIn also supports the consolidation and transference of lessons drawn from SDC supported decentralisation and local governance projects in the past to other actors and institutions. This workshop was organised by LoGIn as a result of:

- Feedback received from a 'Good Practices Workshop' organised by LoGIn in August 2009 in which the need to (i) support direct learning (by Panchayats or from Panchayat to Panchayat), and (ii) to assess the strength of collectives of elected representatives to amplify voices from the field was explicitly articulated.
- An interest expressed by Chattisgarh State Institute of Rural Development to the different experiences in federating elected women leaders.
- LoGIn's interest in assessing the interest of federations for tools and methods that can help to gather evidence and generate data for advocacy.

About the Workshop

- Objectives of the workshop were:
  - ➢ To understand the present status of federations in different states;
  - ➢ To understand the current issues and challenges as well as the strategies deployed by the women federations to address these challenges;
  - ➢ To explore possibilities of mutual exchange and support (of experience and knowledge) among the women federations.
- *Duration*: The workshop spanned over 2.5 days from the 7th to 9th September 2010.
- *Participants*: The 28 participants included representatives from nine women's federations and the supporting NGOs. Resource persons also participated in the event.
- *Methodology*: A combination of methods was used. The participating federations presented with the aid of power point presentations on a format[1] which was communicated to them prior to the workshop. Small group discussions were held on key issues followed by presentations in the plenary. The participants were supported by a panel of discussants who consolidated the discussions, flagged emerging issues and helped in further reflection.

- **Main areas of discussion were**

Membership/Form/Structure	Vision/Mission/ Mandate	Sustainability
• Nature: is it a movement or organization or collective? • Internal management: leadership, democracy, conflict resolution • Rationale and Criteria for membership • Levels, Scale and coverage • Relations with state, civil society, market and political parties • Gate keepers and Bye laws	• Origin and Dynamics leading to formation • Mandate: supply or demand driven. • Main tasks: capacity building, support, helpline, advocacy. • Main issues: gender, leadership, devolution, governance, development	• Level of autonomy • Source of legitimacy • Performance and effectiveness indicators • Fund raising and Membership contribution • Role of support organization • Strategic plan of growth • Future implications

Key Points Emerging from the Workshop

- All federations present in the workshop emerged with the support of either the state or a civil society organisation. The federations represented in the meeting were extremely diverse in nature in terms of their size, structure, membership criteria, mandate, systems, coverage, etc. Their evolution and the mandate they give themselves is influenced by the socio-political context, status of devolution in the state, extent of political engagement by the Panchayats and the expectations of support institution.
- Most federations emerged in order to provide a support system for women elected representatives and an enabling environment for women's participation in the political sphere.
- Federations in India have primarily played three key roles:
  (i) Identification and redressal of malpractices activities which hinder women's participation (like misuse of no-confidence motion provision).
  (ii) Identification and advocacy against regressive policies (like two-child norm).
  (iii) Creating an enabling environment for elected women to perform their role (orientation, training and exposure visits, peer-learning and on-site support).
- It was agreed that there was no ideal type of federation. Whether, it is an organically evolved federation; a top down

model, a registered body, a loose and open collective or a rule bound formal structure each type has its own set of strengths and challenges.

- On the issue of membership and inclusion, most federations resolved the *membership criterion* very pragmatically. While inclusion of all sections of the community was a concern of all federations in the early stages the charismatic, more vocal and active elected women leaders tend to occupy the leadership space. Many argued that federation were supposed to be for current elected leaders but they have retained a percentage of former elected women leaders who have been very active and influential.
- The issue of managing *internal conflicts* did not get discussed enough in the workshop. It appeared that federations were still in a nascent stage and had quite some homogeneity and singularity of purpose for fundamental conflicts to arise. In cases where friction emerges, the support organisation (non-governmental organisation supporting the federation) plays a significant role in conflict resolution.
- Federations shared that it was important to *demonstrate results and achieve small successes* which were tangible so as to 'incentivise' membership to the federation.
- Most federations saw women *self help groups as allies* and have debated and or made provisions for inclusion of SHG leaders in the federations.

Issues Confronting Federations Relate to

- How to make it truly representative of all elected women leaders (inclusion of elected women from all classes, castes, minorities comes with possibilities of internal conflicts).
- How to place a federation in an environment where increased politicisation of Panchayats is inevitable (preparedness of support institutions to accept this and strategise).
- Growing beyond the support institution.
- Institutionalisation of systems and practices to ensure sustainability.
- How important is registration for an independent identity

and fund raising. On the other hand, to what extent can it curb political freedom and flexibility in work?

- Financial Resources and sustainability.
- Access to know-how on successes of federations in other states.

Needs of the Federations

- Designing indicators of performance and effectiveness.
- Affiliation to a pan-India institution which can provide support for advocacy, which can provide forums for mutual learning and which can facilitate to access knowledge and financial resources.
- Stronger political perspective and a better understanding of grassroots politics.
- A strong well debated out and consultatively developed vision, mission and mandate which strengthens the institution and enables it to function over time beyond the shadow of its support institution.

Further Reflections from the Workshop

Inclusion: Inclusion or exclusion is manifested not just in membership but also in the agenda being set or the mandate that the federation gives itself. A question that the federation needs to be asking itself relates to who is setting the agenda in terms of the concerns on which the federation is focusing. It is felt that women of each tier of Panchayats or women from each section of caste, class have different problems so a common forum can sideline a particular group or a particular problem.

Cooption: While a federation aims at strengthening the leadership of its members, there is always a fear that the strong leaders may jeopardize the federation for their political mileage. As federations spread their outreach, political parties see them as potential allies. How such situations have to be handled, what will be the non-negotiable for a federation are questions that need repeated deliberation within the federation.

Support institutions: It was evident that the only window to the outside world (in terms of resources, know-how, linkages) for the federations is via the support institution. Therefore, the strength and weakness of the support institution in terms of perspectives, outreach, contacts, and resources reflect in the maturity of the federation as well. The support institutions guiding and accompanying the federations do influence:

- Understanding of grassroots party politics and extent of engagement of the federation with this politics
- Linkages at state and national level
- Coverage area and Members
- Vision, Mission and Mandate of the Federation.

Recognition: In India, there are platforms, forums and associations related to decentralisation and local governance at state and national level. They primarily comprise of representation from the civil society, state and recently the corporate sector. Federations have not yet been recognised as units that need to be engaged with. Representations from federations in such platforms have not been sought, neither have the federations.

Documentation: The experience of bringing together women elected representatives in collectives, associations, federations is almost a decade old. But the documentation is limited and it has primarily been on reporting activities. The experience, the lessons, the failures, the processes need to be studied, written about, analysed and shared such that it can be utilised for learning and exchange.

Looking into the Future

Federations of elected women leaders are clearly serving a purpose in political empowerment of women and in strengthening of local self-governments. But not enough investment has been done to nurture them. Federations require support and recognition so they can carve a clear identity; role; trajectory of growth; allies; networks and path (apart from the support institution).

Face to face interaction is regarded as the best means to bring women together and create a sense of collective. However, given the time, distance and cost implications, it may not be the most efficient and sustainable means. Can technology be used to aid some of these challenges? If yes, where and how? Are the support institutions receptive to such ideas? Have there been any experiments? What kind of investment will it require? Can the financial resources of the state and private sector as well as the facilitation skills of the NGOs used to innovate on such lines? How receptive are the state institutions and civil society to the available e-platforms?

The role of women as political leaders in local governments is inherently linked to the issues of decentralisation and devolution in the state. But advocacy for devolution of funds, functions and functionaries which can actually change the fabric of decentralisation and local governance have not been the forte of federations. It is important to explore the potential of federations in influencing larger policy reform.

ANNEXURE

Background Note to the National Workshop

Strengthening Women's Leadership in Local Governments through Collectives and Federations

A Report of SDC

7th to 9th September 2010, Hotel Clarion, New Delhi

Hosted By: Local Governance Initiative South Asia (LoGIn),

A Project of Swiss Agency for Development and Cooperation (SDC) in India

Thematic Context

Local institutions at village level have existed in India traditionally and were vested with significant powers, both executive and judicial. They were known as Panchayats literally meaning 'a collective of five elders' who commanded authority to take decisions on village issues. In some parts of India there was an erosion of the overall functioning of these institutions in the 19th and early 20th century while in other parts they took varied shape like caste-based Panchayats or Panchayats around predominant economic activity. Irrespective of the composition, Panchayats have primarily been institutions hosted by individuals who derived their legitimacy from belonging to a dominant caste, class, gender or religion.

It is only in 1993, that the 73rd and 74th Amendments to the Constitution of India provided the legal basis for Panchayats to take the role of local governments. This was historic amendment bringing direct democracy at the local level, both in the rural and urban areas. The 73rd Amendment provided the legislative framework for the introduction of a three-tier system of elected councils in rural areas in all states of India. It was meant to provide constitutional sanction to establish "democracy at the grassroots level as it is at the state level or national level".

However, a range of issues have been limiting the engagement of communities in the local political sphere. These include:

- Political and bureaucratic resistance to Panchayats.
- Elite capture in Panchayat leadership.
- Lack of clarity on roles, relationships and responsibilities.
- Differentiated pace of political, administrative and fiscal decentralisation within a state as well as across the states.
- Setting up of competing institutions by administrative decree at the village level. The non-binding nature of the recommendations of the State Finance Commissions very frugal devolution of resources to the Panchayats.

The 73rd and 74th Amendments also demonstrated a model of affirmative action validated by the Constitution which offered a unique way of engineering social inclusion through the allocation of reserved seats in local government:

- Mandatory reservation of seats at all three levels for people from Scheduled Castes (SC) and Scheduled Tribes (ST) in proportion of the population. This was further amended to include Other Backward Classes (OBC).
- Mandatory reservation of at least one-third of all seats for women.

This has translated into a huge number from marginalised communities occupying positions of leadership in local governments.

Women and Local Governance in India

Background

In India feudalism and patriarchy have been the underlying reasons restricting women from being equal citizens of the political society. There are several overt and subtle norms and values that suppress the identity and individuality of women. In the name of honour and shame, women do not have the same freedom to access public life. Apart from the caste based restrictions, women shoulder the burden of gender based restrictions, which cut across every caste and class in India. They are expected to walk with their heads down, speak softly or not speak at all in public forums, give primacy to their domestic obligations and avoid contact or interaction with men.

The role of social movements, especially women's movements, in securing substantive political representation is underexplored. In India, by and large, women's movements have shied away from engaging with political parties and the demand for greater political representation of women at the local level has not come from the movement. The passing of the Constitutional Amendment with one-third reservations for women was a top down process which was not necessarily backed by the preparedness on the ground. It brought nearly 1.2 million women in local Panchayats as elected leaders. These numbers are huge and so are the challenges. Bringing more women into local level decision-making is one set of issues. However, sustaining women in power represents another set of issues for which other mechanisms are necessary. Affirmative action is a necessary but not sufficient condition to overcome the rigid social and cultural barriers that women face and which disallow their participation in the public sphere.

Challenges

- Lack of orientation and training after resuming their position. Apathy from the government officials, bureaucrats and Police Interference or restriction from family members or caste/class leaders. Masculine nature of public politics: money, muscle, alcoholism.

- *Lack of skills*: reading, writing, communication, management etc.
- *Lack of information*: schemes, budgets, maps etc.
- Low confidence levels and fear of the unknown.
- *Lack of support systems*: legal, social, economic, etc. Fact that there are not many role models.
- Low level of motivation.
- *Issue of caste*: the upper caste women apparently enjoy the caste hierarchy but have to curtail her public life and identity in the name of family pride. On the other hand, a lower caste woman, who may have the freedom to go out in public, tends to face assault from upper caste men who justify their violent behaviour as their caste based right.
- *Issue of poverty*: women belonging to poor, landless families find it very challenging to take on their leadership roles due to economic pressures.
- Dual work load of home and office which puts a lot of pressure on women leaders.

Further, women's historical exclusion from local government means that they do not have access to many of the informal networks that sustain and reproduce the institutions and social practices that make up local governance institutions and practices. Over the past fifteen years, the debate has centred on the following issues:

- Women's access to the political mainstream at the local level.
- The support systems that women require when they are on their path of leadership.
- Incentive of political parties to groom young women leaders at the local level.
- Role of the state in securing the substantive representation of women: Besides quotas what other state initiated measures are necessary to ensure that political parties and the electorate engage with women candidates?
- Models of capacity building, support system in India and the related challenges.

Needs of Elected Women Leaders

Election as a representative is the first step, albeit a critical one for an elected woman leader to discharge her public responsibilities. Given the fact that most women are coming into public life for the first time, if their voice is to be sustained and reinforced across all levels of government, then women's political participation at the local level requires support and integration into broader political processes. Both as effective leaders and for advocacy, women require technical skills and support. Experience of organisations that have worked with elected women representatives point out that elected women leaders are able to best discharge their responsibilities when provided with:

- Basic orientation within the first few months of resuming their position.
- Skill, information and knowledge based trainings.
- Forums to meet and engage with each other.
- Forums to interact with government officials and bureaucrats.
- Legal and institutional support.

Federations of Elected Women Leaders

An emerging process of supporting elected women representatives has been the formation of "federations", at block, district and even the state level. This has come about from various sources—some through the initiative of the state government while others through civil society initiatives: some of them are effectively functioning while others are either dormant or ineffective. However, there are now multiple attempts towards creating federations across the country and it seems to be an accepted method to build on the base to support women leaders in public life. The Union Government has also sought to give impetus to federations through the Panchayat Mahila Shakti Abhiyan.

Primarily the formation of collectives was an attempt to address:

- Issues of corruption and lack of work ethics among the dominant leaders and government functionaries.
- Hostile environment which make it difficult for women to participate, speak and play their designated roles.

Federations of elected members, where they exist, have been seen to be highly political and male dominated with women leaders hardly getting a chance to be visible or expressing their views. Certain common practices related to formation and support of federations that can be discerned across states and time include:

- NGOs with a mass based network creating platforms for elected women to come together and form collectives.
- Collectives supported to meet regularly and discuss common issues.
- Consolidation of the concerns followed by creating forums to articulate those concerns.
- Facilitate formation of associations and federations as support base for elected women.
- Federations develop a structure, rules, membership system, specific activities etc.
- Federations play a support and capacity building role during pre-election, during election, post-election and in the five year cycle of elected woman leader.

Background to the Workshop

The Swiss Agency for Development and Cooperation (SDC) in India has been supporting programmes of the state and civil society aimed at strengthening local governance and decentralisation. 'Local Governance Initiative (LoGIn) South Asia' is a project of SDC promoting south-south and north-south knowledge exchange on decentralisation and local governance.

In August 2009, LoGIn organised a Good Practices Workshop where SDC supported experiences in India on decentralisation and local governance were presented and scope for mutual learning and exchange were discussed. One of the recommendations of the participant group was the need to support direct learning (Panchayat to Panchayat) and strengthen collectives of elected representatives to amplify voices from the field. Since then LoGIn has supported exchange visits between Panchayats in India and has also been interested to support platforms for advocacy on decentralisation and local governance in India. Women's federations provide an opportunity to see how elected leaders come together to learn from each other, support each other and take their common concerns to the state or national level.

In June 2010, SIRD Chattisgarh, nodal agency for capacity development of elected representatives of PRIs in Chhattisgarh, shared with LoGIn, the need to compliment efforts of capacity building with allied programmes. With the three batches of elected leaders over the past 15 years coming in, there has been a concern that training alone is not sufficient for developing capacity. In order to support them to voice their concern and priorities in Panchayat meetings and effectively influence the decision-making process, the State of Chhattisgarh is interested to support formation of federation of elected women.

Rationale for the Workshop

Capitalise Experiences

Across India, there has been considerable effort around collectivising and federating elected women leaders at the grassroots. There is a need to understand these processes and how they have helped in strengthening decentralisation and local governance. This will not only help the existing federations in horizontal learning but also suggest how federations can be formed in states which do not have such collectives already.

Exploring Potential for Common Advocacy Platforms

It is increasingly felt that the nature of the future course of decentralisation and local governance in India (structure, systems, policies etc.) should be anchored by Panchayat representatives and functionaries who are grappling and coping with the everyday issues related to local self-government institutions. This calls for common platforms of advocacy of federations in India and support to help them consolidate as well as articulate recommendations for policies.

Sustainability

It is known that when the real needs are a basis of development activities then it creates greater ownership amongst the stakeholders as well as ensures more rigour in the operations. The federations could provide a strong base for mutual learning, support and advocacy which is likely to be sustainable as it will represent the real needs at the grassroots.

Objectives of the Workshop

The purpose of the workshop is to facilitate the exchange of experiences on creation and functioning of the federations of EWR of PRIs and draw lessons that could be used for strengthening their role and leadership capacities through creation of federation for effective implementation of decentralised governance programmes for economic development and social justice:

1. To understand the present status of federations in different states.
2. To understand the current issues and challenges and strategies deployed to address these challenges.
3. To explore possibilities of mutual exchange and support (of experience and knowledge).

Issues to be Covered during the Workshop

- **Membership/Form/Structure of existing federations and related issues:**
  - ➢ Rationale of membership.
  - ➢ *Criteria*: fixed, flexible, current elected leaders, former elected leaders.
  - ➢ Scale and coverage.
  - ➢ Gate keepers.
  - ➢ Nature of the structure.
  - ➢ Bye laws.
- **Vision/Mission/Mandate of existing federations and related issues:** Origin and Dynamics leading to formation
  - ➢ *Evolution*
  - ➢ *Agenda setting*: capacity building, support, helpline, advocacy etc. Mandate is supply driven or demand driven
  - ➢ *Nature*: programme, movement or organisation

- **Sustainability**
  - Fund raising
  - Membership contribution
  - Role of support organisation
  - Level of autonomy
  - Source of legitimacy
  - Strategic plan of
  - growth
  - Future implications

About the Participants

Resource Support Centre for Development, Maharashtra: RSCD is facilitating six regional networking bodies comprising of 204 development actors across 31 districts of the State of Maharashtra and in 7 districts in the State of Rajasthan. The values promoted are collectivism, bottom up planning, decentralised administration and decision-making process, accountability and transparency, advocacy intervention for social change.

Mahila Rajsatta Andolan, Maharashtra: MRA works in 26 districts, 78 blocks, with 1800 EWRs of Maharashtra; through various intervention strategies like—Advocacy, Organising Training Programmes, Crisis Support, Documentation, and Dissemination of Information to Elected Women Representatives (EWRs). It has played an effective role in network building, capacity building, and creating support systems to ensure Women's active, efficient, and effective participation in the local self-governance.

Kutch Mahila Vikas Sangathan, Gujarat: KMVS is a collective group of rural women based in the western state of Gujarat. There are over 4000 members, with at least 1200 being traditional artisans. KMVS has a Panchayat Cell called Suhasini which primarily works with elected women leaders in Kutch.

Mahila Swaraj Abhiyan, Gujarat: MSA is a state wide informal network of 40 Non-government Organisations (NGOs) working on women's issues in 13 districts of Gujarat. MSA is coordinating, providing direction and support to a state wide movement for, building a collective identity and strengthening women's participation in political processes.

SUTRA, Himachal Pradesh: Society for Social Uplift Through Rural Action was established in 1977 with the support from SWRC, Tilonia. SUTRA, through its network of small voluntary organisations, works with village based Mahila Mandals and women representatives of Gram Panchayats spread across 7 districts of Himachal Pradesh. It also works on policy at advocacy issues at the state and national level.

The Hunger Project, Delhi is a part of The Hunger Project (THP) global, a non-profit, strategic organisation committed to the sustainable end of world hunger. The Hunger Project has been active in India since 1984 and currently works across 10 states. The Hunger Project's approach of mobilising people for self-reliant action, empowering women as key change agents and engaging with local government is culminated in one comprehensive strategy, the Panchayati Raj Campaign.

Singamma Sreenivasan Foundation, Karnataka: SSF has been working on political and economic empowerment of women in nine districts of Karnataka in collaboration with state government, Unifem and Janaagraha.

Centre for World Solidarity, Andhra Pradesh (SWS): Set up in 1992, CWS works on issues of rights, livelihood and governance. CWS initiated its Panchayati Raj Initiatives programme in 2000 in Andhra Pradesh through 15 NGOs. The programme focused on Pre-election Voter Awareness Campaign (PEVAC), capacity building to elected representatives, preparation and dissemination of IEC materials, initiating networks of representatives and establishing linkages with organisations/institutions involved in empowering PRIs. The programme is active currently in Andhra Pradesh, Orissa, Jharkhand, and Pondicherry.

Astha, Rajasthan: Formed in 1986, Astha has been working on issues of rights and justice of the marginalised across Rajasthan on issues of tribal self-rule, panchayati raj and women's empowerment.

Gandhigram, Tamil Nadu: Found in 1956, Gandhigram is a deemed university offering Masters and PhD programmes in science and arts. It is known for its contribution to research and publications on local governance and women's leadership.

Sakhi, Kerala: Sakhi is a women's resource centre based in Kerala. They have been actively engaged in promoting women's participation in local governance. Capacity development, gender budgeting and

VAW related interventions form part of their work. As part of developing the capacity of women leaders, Sakhi has been associated with creating networks of EWRs in Thiruvananthapuram and Kollam districts. Sakhi is currently focusing on an intense process of working in 9 Panchayats in Thiruvananthapuram district with an idea to help in the overall development process of the Panchayats with emphasis on women's development.

Association of Local Governance of India (ALGI), Delhi: ALGI is an association set-up to promote Panchayati Raj in India. It acts as an advocacy and influence group promoting the interests of local governments and the decentralisation process in India. It also conducts research and provides specialised services to the members on matters related to local government policies and programmes mobilise and augment the efforts of local government in obtaining their constitutional and legal entitlements. The elected representatives of local government institutions, experts in the field of local government and institutions working in the field of local governments are members of ALGI coming from all-over India—all the States and Union Territories

Ministry of Panchayati Raj, Delhi (Panchayat Mahila Shakti Abhiyan): PMSA is a scheme implemented through the Ministry of Panchayati Raj. It is meant for the Elected Women Representatives (EWRs) to build their confidence and capacity so that they get over the institutional, societal and political constraints that prevent them from active participation in rural local self-government. A core element of the scheme is to promote networks of EWRs. As of January 2010, 22 States have formed the Core Committee and organised the State Level Sammelans. 9 State Support Centres have been established under the scheme. (Andhra Pradesh, Chhattisgarh, Goa, Himachal Pradesh, Madhya Pradesh, Sikkim, Kerala, West Bengal and Andaman & Nicobar Island). 11 States have been conducted training sensitisation programme under the scheme. (Andhra Pradesh, Arunachal Pradesh, Chhattisgarh, Goa, Himachal Pradesh, Madhya Pradesh, Manipur, Kerala, Assam, Andaman and Nicobar Island and Sikkim). Rs. 2.4 crores was sanctioned by MoPR for this scheme in 2009-10 (Rs. 2.02 crores in 2007-08, Rs. 2.45 crores in 2008-09).

ANNEXURE

A REPORT

LOCAL GOVERNANCE INITIATIVE SOUTH ASIA

Knowledge Exchange Programme on Local Governance

Local Go Regional

National Workshop Strengthening Women Leadership in Local Governments through Collectives and Federations 7th to 9th September 2010; Hotel Clarion, New Delhi.

PART 1
BACKGROUND AND CONTEXT OF THE WORKSHOP

Experience over the past 15 years has shown that elected women representatives face significant hurdles in exercising their authority and role as panchayat representatives. An emerging process of supporting Elected Women Representatives (EWRs) has been the formation of "federations", at block, district and even the state level.

This has come about from various sources—some through the initiative of the state government while others through civil society initiatives. The Union Government has also sought to give impetus to federations of EWRs through the Panchayat Mahila Shakti Abhiyan.

While some of the federations have been successful, others are either dormant or have become dysfunctional. They have operated at different scales, some at block level, others at district and a few have been able to grow till the state level.

Currently several attempts towards creating EWR federations are visible across the country and it has become an accepted means to build on the emergence of women in political life. This in turn is enabled to a large extent by at least 1/3rd reservations of all seats in local governments for women provided through the 73rd Constitutional Amendment.

The need to have an understanding on the current efforts in federating women leaders was brought out in a previous workshop held by SDC-LoGIn in August 2009. Follow up recommendations emerging from the workshop urged donors and the government to support such federations of elected representatives. This also led-LoGIn to consider building capacities of elected representatives on various themes through existing federations: possible themes under discussion have been functional assignments/activity mapping, gender budgeting, and budget tracking. While this formed the backdrop, the impetus for the current workshop came from the request of State Institute of Rural Development (SIRD), Chhattisgarh to support a consultation to discuss learning emerging from efforts of forming federations/collectives of elected women representatives. Chattisgarh has had its Panchayat elections across the state and is looking at federations of elected women as a viable and sustainable base for long-term support and capacity building.

LoGIn invited a number of Federations along with their support institutions to share their experiences and learnings. The following pages seek to capture the deliberations during the workshop.

Objectives of this Workshop were to–

- Understand the present status of federations (membership,

current activities and priorities) Map out common concerns and challenges and share strategies deployed to address these challenges.
- Explore if there is interest and scope for mutual learning.

Schedule of the Workshop

- The workshop was spread over three days (refer to the workshop schedule in Appendix 1).
- The first day devoted to the sharing of experiences of various federations of EWRs.[1]
- The second day to collectively understand the learnings that could be distilled from these experiences.
- The third day was used to understand the Union Government's approach to such federation building and to another effort towards creating a pan-India body for elected representatives and other interested parties in local governments called Association of Local Governments Institutions (ALGI). An assessment of needs of EWR Federations and follow-up was also undertaken before closing the workshop.

About the Participants

Participants in the workshop came from ten states across the country and comprised of Elected Women Representatives and people representing civil society organisations supporting Federations. The group comprised of nine federations/collectives of elected women representatives, 9 CSOs, and from the Gandhigram Rural University and the SIRD Chhattisgarh team[2]. The workshop adopted the use of discussants to help focus the discussions by clarifying, challenging and reminding the group of relevant experiences and flagging key issues. Discussants included Dr. R.K. Singh, the Director of SIRD Chhattisgarh, Ms. Aleyamma Vijayan, from SAKHI, Kerala and Dr. Joy Elamon, from the UNDP Solutions Exchange Decentralisation Community of Practice.

PART 2
PRESENTATIONS

Presentations were limited to 20 minutes followed by a discussion of another 25 minutes after that. Issues needing more deliberation were noted and flagged for further discussion. At the end of the day, the flagged issues were categorised and proposed for discussion on Day 2.

> *This section presents a synopsis of the presentation and discussions on day one. Please note that the proceedings as reported include the presentations made by the participants, their response to queries of clarification and in some cases, material from the information shared at the workshop. Also, the presentation of the Goa PMSA was made on Day 2 but has been reported here to maintain the flow of the report.*

2.1 Mahila Rajsatta Andolan, Maharashtra[3]

Introduction

The Mahila Rajsatta Andolan (MRA) works across the state of Maharashtra and has a presence in 26 of the 35 districts of the state. MRA was built on a platform created by civil society organisations in

Maharashtra to promote women in politics. MRA is an unregistered group with established by-laws and a clear leadership. There are no plans to get the group a formal identity through registration as it is believed that advocacy issues can be better articulated through such a grouping. MRA slogan of "*Vote Hamara, Raj Hamara*" (my vote, my rule) establishes its political orientation of ensuring participation of women in the electoral process as well as their engagement with governance.

Structure and Coverage

Sixty-two NGOs continue to provide support to the MRA through training and information. Some NGOs also provide crisis support. Resource and Support Centre for Development (RSCD) plays the facilitating and coordinating role for these support organisations.

Coverage of MRA

Region	District	Tehsil	Gaon Shakha	Focus Gaon
Marathwada	8	21	40	160
West Maharashtra	5	16	26	100
Konkan	2	6	12	40
Nagpur	6	23	11	120
Amravati	5	22	23	100
Total	**26**	**88**	**112**	**520**

STRUCTURE OF MRA

MRA has units at the village, tehsil, district and State level. The Women's Front comprising non-elected women support the Elected Panchayat Women Front across all three tiers (Panchayati Raj Aaghadi). The State Council comprises 22 members (4 from Disctrict level, 8 from Tehsils, 5 Regional leaders, 4 from PRI front and 1 state committee member). Currently around 2000 EWRs are members of MRA with total membership coming 14,000 women. Each member contributes Rs.10 and EWRs contribute Rs.100 annually respectively as fees to MRA. Currently, 40 per cent of the State Council members are nominated with goal of making all positions elected over time.

The Hunger Project and Actionaid India have provided support to RSCD to facilitate the MRA. Internal resource mobilisation primarily occurs through sale of publications and collection of membership fees. Currently, 10 per cent of the resources are being internally generated with plans of expansion of the local resource mobilisation through fellowships for EWRs.

Activities

A network of NGOs supported the emergence of women in the panchayats by promoting them to participate in the electoral process (year 2000). With EWRs coming out of this process, MRA supported the Gram Sabha Gourav Abhiyan—to encourage the participation of women and other marginalised people in the Gram Sabhas (year 2002). By 2003, the EWRs and CSO partners had started discussing the need for building alliances and a PRI front was established in 2006. Current intervention strategies and activities of MRA are around:

- Organisation and Alliance Building to deepen the MRA
  - ➢ Strengthen the village unit
  - ➢ Expansion of EWR Membership
- Policy Advocacy—focusing on policy execution and policy change.
- Capacity Building interventions—through leadership workshops, Training trainers and BOSS course (which covers the essential aspects of panchayats: Budgets Orders Schemes Services) Publications.

Unlike other States, Maharashtra does not have elections across the state in a five year cycle. Rather elections are a continuous process being held in one location after another (though the term for each seat is 5 years). This also has implications for the patterns of membership of the MSA as EWRs are coming in and retiring from their positions all the time. Former EWRs continue to engage with MRA but more importantly as trainers for the new set of EWRs.

Achievements

- MRA sees its key achievement in raising consciousness of the members and understanding of their rights, enabling changes in lives of the people, policy advocacy towards better local governance and rights of elected members and building an effective organisation.
- A government order provisioning for free state transport bus pass for women representatives at all three tiers.
- Obtaining clarification from the state government to support the Women President's right to hoist the National Flag on Independence Day.
- Now there is a pre-requisite of 3/4th majority to pass a no-confidence motion against elected women leaders. This was a very important policy level change because most active women leaders had lost their seats because of false accusations and no-confidence motions could be easily secured and passed against them.
- A government order provisioning for women's Gram Sabha prior to the general.

Challenges and Lessons

- Youth support has to be mobilised to widen the base.
- Study the ground reality before action—Creating village specific status paper of women, village power processes and village specific party mapping has created a micro-level understanding of issues faced by women. This along with political campaign for Mahila Gram Sabhas (exclusive village meetings of women) has resulted in increased participation of women in governance processes.
- Address internal conflicts — MRA is a growing, dynamic body with members often having divergent opinions leading to internal conflicts. Conflicts usually arise while taking political positions and there is debate and heated discussion among the members. A Conflict Resolution Committee has been created to help resolve issues. Tensions also arise on issues around party/ Caste/ Class and efforts are made to build

consensus amongst the members. MRA engages with all EWRs and does not differentiate women based on their party affiliations. It sees education of members about the political parties as important.

2.2 Tamil Nadu Association of Women Presidents of Panchayat Government[4]

Introduction

It is observed by the Gandhigram Rural University that over the years, local NGOs in Tamil Nadu have shown limited interest in working with Panchayats in a sustained manner. The Dravidian political movement raised issues of women rights which lead to creation of a space for women in public life in Tamil Nadu. Political engagement of women in Tamil Nadu, especially at the Panchayats level, has been significant. EWR collectives in Tamil Nadu emerged as a result of women requiring support to negotiate with government officials and deal with male colleagues/leaders. Formation of local level initiatives of EWR collectives was an organic process had organically started and over the years there has been debate on how the leadership issue needs to be managed in these collectives.

Structure and Coverage

- As the Federation took shape, EWRs elected at the Block level wanted to be part of the process. However, the Federation did not allow them membership on the grounds that they are elected on the basis of a Political Party and would feel constrained in taking independent decisions.
- The Dalit Gram Panchayat leaders, on the other hand, decided to form a separate Federation to highlight specific issues confronting them. Both the Dalit and the broader federation continued to co-operate and work with each other.
- These federations got visibility when the local Tamil newspapers and Tamil Nadu based media houses started highlighting their activities. With visibility and growth, the Federation decided to get registered in 2002-03 and now has a membership of around 1200 Gram Panchayat Presidents.

- Participation of the women ward members in the Federation was considered but it was felt that the Federation needs to consolidate all the Panchayat Presidents first and was thus deferred. The structure of the federation is loose with the President and Secretary being chosen through a consensus.

Main Activities

- Creating avenues for capacity building like training, workshops, exposure visits. Joint efforts for Advocacy.
- Regular interaction with bureaucrats and politicians.
- Engaging with media to make the efforts of the federation visible.

Achievements

- With established leadership emerging through the Federation, political parties started engaging with the Federation. Some of the prominent leaders moved to political parties.
- Federation demanded two term reservation for reserved seats, opposed two-child norm when it came up for discussion in the state, and influenced the state to issue a GO to the BDOs to help the meetings of the Federation at the block level.
- The Federation has effectively engaged with the bureaucracy and politicians to advocate for better implementation of development programmes.

Challenges

- *Interference of political parties:* Political parties saw the Federation as both a threat and an opportunity and started engaging with the leadership.
- *Interference of NGOs*
- *Lure of higher posts*: Engagement with political parties and being effective leaders at the gram panchayat level, the leaders were tempted to contest for higher positions. While this was good for the individual leaders, the Federation has to deal with losing effective leaders. Finding the right balance of

providing minimum support by the facilitating organisations that they can stand on their own over the maximum period. Federation should be able to lead from the front and decide their own agenda.

Lessons

Information support through helpline is important and mechanisms of regular two way information across the members. Gandhigram interventions as a facilitating organisation were made in the following areas:

- Capacity building of federations
- Information support
- Hand-holding support
- Perspective building
- Regular refresher training
- Interface and forward and backward linkages with the government and community.

The Gandhigram Rural Institute, the support organisation sought to support this growth in a systematic manner, with capacity building on roles and functions combined with leadership development and engagement with the media. Other organisations also supported this process. However, with differing perspectives being offered, the emerging collectives formed into separate federations across Tamil Nadu.

2.3 Panchayat Mahila Manch, Gujarat[5]

Introduction

Mahila Swaraj Abhiyan (a network of NGOs to work on strengthening women's participation in governance) was set-up in 1994. A large meeting was hosted in 1997 to bring together NGOs and women leaders from 16 districts of Gujarat. MSA as a registered Trust and Society brought together 27 NGOs members. It has cluster level units to keep a visible presence at the grassroots level. It works on local issues emerging from EWRs by influencing policies at state level to strengthen women's position in Panchayati Raj.

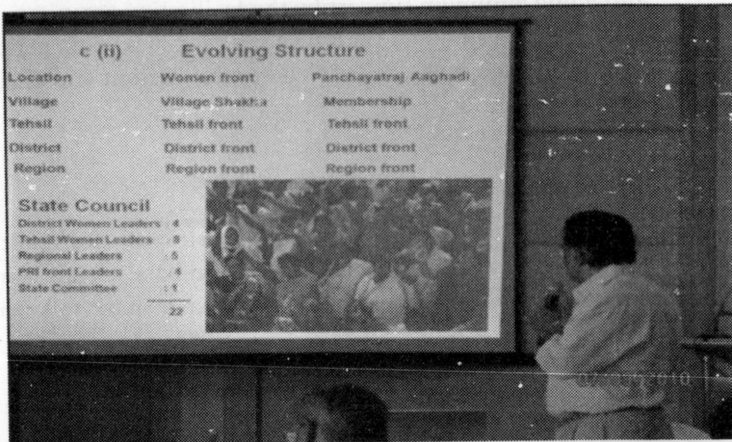

Panchayat Mahila Manch (PMM) is an unregistered forum and is a programme of the MSA. Its objectives are to:

- Identify and address gaps in gender-sensitivity of local government functions and functionaries.
- Identify and carry forward the needs and concerns of EWRs which affect their full functioning as effective leadership in local self-governing institutions.
- Identify and address development issues for women and marginalised populations towards legitimising their political voice.

Structure

- PMM is a membership based forum with 75 per cent of the members being EWRs from the Gram Panchayats and 25 per cent being local women leaders comprising former EWRs and Self-Help Group (SHG) leaders. SHG women are critical to mobilise other women for Gram Sabhas and it was felt that they should have formal membership in the PMM.
- The PMM is working across 6 districts of Gujarat currently. The selection of districts was done on the basis of population; caste based discrimination as well as representation of local support NGOs.
- MSA focuses on South Gujarat where a large number of Tribal communities reside and fall under the Schedule VI areas where PESA (Panchayat Extension to Scheduled Areas) is not being implemented adequately.
- 43 block level Forums have a membership of 1955 women leaders. There are 120 members in the 4 district level forums.
- Sabarkhanta, Surendranagar, Panchmahal and Dahod have district as well as block Forums while Kutch and Bhavnagar only have block level forums.
- The Block Manch in Bhavnagar is registered while others are not registered. By-laws exist for each manch and members pay a fee of Rs. 50 annually.
- At the block level, monthly meetings are held by the Manch with an annual district level meeting.
- 10 to 15 members are elected from the Gram Panchayats to the Block Manch. These members choose the district level committee members.
- At the current stage, the Manch have formulated their by-laws and hold the annual meeting.
- The Annual General Body decides the activities and reviews the progress of the previous year's activities.

Activities

Panchayat Mahila Manch (PMM) activities towards increasing women political participation in panchayats include:

- Pre-Election Voters Awareness Campaign (PEVAC)
- Meeting at district and block levels.
- Capacity building through trainings and exposure visits.
- Identification of advocacy issues.
- Advocacy events and district level campaigns.
- Follow-up with state government.

The block level capacity building interventions are focused on Panchayati Raj issues while at the district level additional inputs focus on value based issues on themes around democracy, gender etc.

The Future actions of the PMM include creating model panchayats, expansion of the PMM to other districts of the state and creating a state level manch as a union of EWRs with representation from Dalit, Muslim and tribal communities.

Achievements

- The Manchs have served as an effective platform for EWRs to talk and voice their concern as they generate a sense of solidarity as well as giving directions and energy to the capabilities of the EWRs. They have been successfully able to communicate the administrative and policy level problems at three tiers to the administration. While advocating, the PMM engages with the media to highlight issues.
- The Manch have taken up policy level issues:
  - ➢ Changing rules for no-confidence motions in the State Panchayati Raj Act where the motion is presented and voted upon by the elected panchayat members rather than the Gram Sabha.
  - ➢ Against the imposition of the "two-child norm" for Panchayats that impacts EWRs adversely.
  - ➢ Against the recent amendment to make at least Class Xth level education as a qualification to contest elections.
  - ➢ Regarding participation of women in Gram Sabhas.
  - ➢ Implementation of PESA.

Challenges

- Since the 2005-06 elections, membership fee has been erratic in all Manch except in Bhavnagar (the only registered Manch).

- PMM still requires help from support organisations in planning their activities and to raise funds. However, the need to generate local funding for their activities is already being discussed in the Manch.

Lessons

The mainstream electoral process of buying votes was visible in some places during the last elections. While this issue was raised and resolved in the subsequent annual general body meeting of PMM, it shows that the values of leadership are very difficult to challenge.

2.4 The Andhra Pradesh Panchayat Elected Women Representatives Association[6]

Introduction

Andhra Pradesh has always had a history of Panchayat members unions. Sarpanchs (President of Village Panchayats) Federations, Mandal (block/intermediary panchayats) Parishad Federations at the state and district levels have existed. Centre for World Solidarity felt the need to engage in this process despite the fact that such federations existed when they entered PRI strengthening programme in 2000. The programme focused on capacity building of SC, ST and women representatives. Networks were formed at the Mandal, Local Area and state level to address issues related to Panchayats through advocacy and lobbying. A state level network with linkages with all existing unions/federations was created with the help of Centre for World Solidarity (CWS). CWS continued to strengthen the network in its operational area and two mandal level networks (one exclusively for women) each in nine mandals were formed.

Structure

- Centre for World Solidarity (CWS) was identified as Nodal agency for the PMEYSA (Panchayat Mahila Evam Yuva Shakti Abhiyan—see box below) for Andhra Pradesh—where one of the objectives is to form a Federation of EWRs across the state.
- The Federation was initiated during the State Level Sammelan in January 2008 and *ad hoc* district level committees formed immediately after leading to a state level Association on March 2008. The Association was registered in 2009 under the Society Registration Act, Andhra Pradesh as "The Andhra Pradesh Panchayat Elected Women Representatives Association".
- Its coverage is the entire state and it has a 22 member Executive Body with representation from across the state.
- Mobilisation for the federation was done through invitation to the District Panchayats who in turn requested for representation from the LAC and mandal levels respectively. 15 of the 22 Districts responded.
- Financial support for Federation building under the scheme is Rs. 25,000 being released in 2008-09 and Rs. 40,000 for 2010-11. In addition, CWS covers the travel costs of the federation members, while APARD (the State Training Institute in AP) stepped in to cover the boarding and lodging costs.

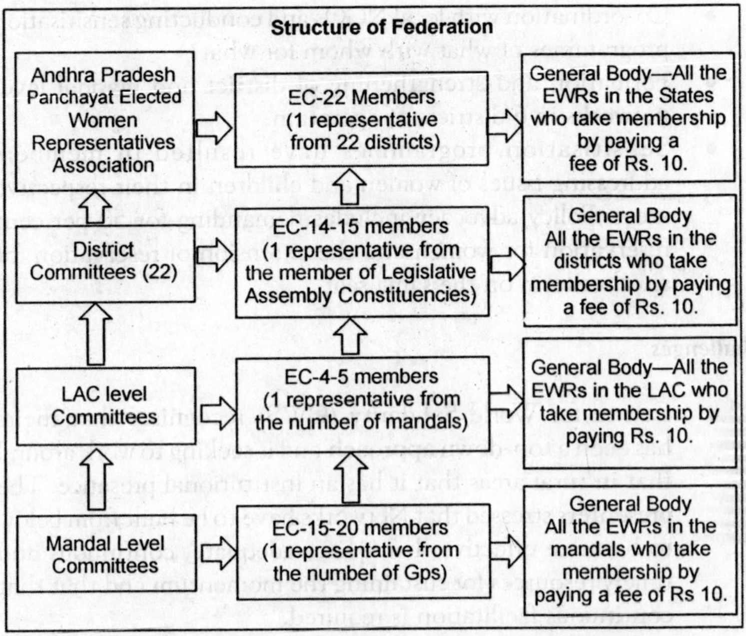

Structure of Federation

PANCHAYAT MAHILA EVAM YUVA SHAKTI ABHIYAN (PMEYSA)

The scheme is implemented through the Ministry of Panchayati Raj. It is meant for the Elected Women Representatives (EWRs) to build their confidence and capacity so that they get over the institutional, societal and political constraints that prevent them from active participation in rural local self-government. A core element of the scheme is to promote networks of EWRs. As of January 2010, 22 States have formed the Core Committee and organised the State Level Sammelans. 9 State Support Centres have been established under the scheme. In 11 States, sensitisation training programmes have been conducted under the scheme.

Activities and Achievements

Current activities of the APEWR Association, being done in areas where CWS works includes:

- Co-ordination with local NGOs and conducting sensitisation programmes of what with whom for what?
- Formation and strengthening of district and mandal level networks in 6 districts of operation.
- Sensitisation programmes have resulted in members addressing issues of women and children in their respective areas. Policy advocacy includes demanding for 50 per cent reservation for women and the extension of reservation for another term on the same seat.

Challenges

- Centre for World Solidarity (CWS) recognises that theirs has been a **top-down approach** and is seeking to work around that in rural areas that it has an institutional presence. The presenters stressed that Networks have to be built from below to be more effective. It requires adequate, continuous and timely resources for sustaining the momentum and that that continuous facilitation is required.
- Attendance in meetings and creating a sense of ownership among the members is another issue along with the limited resources available. However, the Federation has been able to generate an annual membership fee of 100 Rupees from the EWRs and a separate bank account has been opened.
- Sustaining the interests of the members after their term expires in June 2011 is another challenge.

The Federation seeks to expand through engaging with EWRs and orienting them on democratic decentralisation, value of votes, reservations and leadership qualities, among others. Identification of potential candidates to contest elections is also among the future plans.

2.5 Panch-Sarpanch Association, Rajasthan[7]

Introduction

The Panch-Sarpanch Association, Rajasthan is a Federation of EWRs operating at the Block level in Rajasthan. The Block serves as the primary unit. The association supports women in handling the challenges that come with the position of leadership in local panchayats. The association aims to promote decentralisation of grass root level democratic system and create a support system for women to exercise their rights in private and public space. The objectives of the Panch-Sarpanch Association, Rajasthan are to:

- Practically increase the leadership of women at every level in the panchayats.
- Develop political awareness among women of poor, marginalised and Dalit section of the society.
- Ensure timely implementation of legal structural process of Panchayati Raj (local self-government).
- Empower village assembly, come to common consensus and increase participation of women in the village assembly.
- Work for ensuring legal rights of Panch-Sarpanch.
- Advocate for policy change in favour of women.
- Encourage the decentralisation of powers.

Structure

- The association was set-up in October 2005 as a permanent organisation.
- It is currently functional across 63 blocks in 22 districts of Rajasthan.
- The membership comprises of Ward members and Sarpanchs in the Gram Panchayats, with 30 per cent former EWRs invited as members.
- Currently membership is limited to EWRs from the Gram Panchayat level so that there is uniformity. Accepting membership from EWRs at the other two tiers will be considered once the Association is firmly established itself.
- A network of support organisations across these blocks and at the state capital was also created. It is called the Panchayati Raj Sahyog Sangh (PRSS) comprising of 43 NGOs. As part of the PRSS, NGOs support maintenance of records, capacity building and facilitating meetings at the initial stages.

Members pay a fee of Rupees 21 annually and fill in a membership form. A Block Co-ordination Committee of 10-15 members co-ordinates activities in the block and there is a 45 member State Level Committee. While the Association does not have any funds apart from membership, the support organisation helps them raise resources locally and also provide training and logistics support. Local NGOs keep up engagement with the members while the block committee of 10-15 keeps meeting as and when required. Block level Co-ordination committee calls meeting and makes agenda based on emerging issues.

Activities

- At the regional level, the Association has supported its members in organising gram and ward sabhas, building consensual decision-making, providing updated information related to Government Orders as well as initiating processes of sensitisation of Secretary of Gram Panchayats and other elected representatives.
- Activities at the state level include:
  - Advocacy at the state level and dialogue with Ministers towards decentralisation of powers as well as around raising honorarium of elected representatives.
  - Press conferences of emerging issues.
  - Organise a State Level Convention once in two years and an annual regional convention. Establishing support unit at the block and district level.

Achievements

Achievements observed over the past years include:

- The development of confidence in EWRs and chairing their meetings and increased participation in panchayat meetings.
- The EWRs now have an identity at the Block level and the officials recognise and engage with them, including being invited for programmes at the district level.
- With the development of broader perspective and learning

from each other, the members feel more assertive and have started taking up issues such as girl child education, effective implementation of social security schemes; mitigation of violence against women; ensuring food security, education, water and sanitation, basic needs and seeking equality of opportunity and decision-making in Panchayats.

- A demand for 50 per cent reservation was made by the association since 2007, but it would be difficult to ascribe the success of the Government creating 50 per cent reservations for women to the Association directly.

Lessons and Challenges

How to deal with political parties: With 50 per cent reservation of women in Panchayats, more women will occupy positions of leadership. As a result of which, political parties are feeling the need to engage with women. Panch-Sarpanch Association, Rajasthan has to develop strategies to engage with the penetration political parties in local areas.

Expanding Outreach: Future Plans of the Association include expansion to a 100 blocks in Rajasthan. New members are being oriented after the recent Panchayat elections in the State and Block

Level Coordinating Committees will be oriented. Empowerment of the State level Committee to effectively take up issues independently is being promoted. Strategy towards making the Association self-sustaining is being developed. Outreach through a website is under consideration and there is a vision to have a national level association.

2.6 Stree Suchana Sangama[8] Karnataka

Introduction

The Singamma Srenivasan Foundation (SSF) undertook the development of Federations of elected women representatives across four states of Karnataka, Kerala, Andhra Pradesh and Tamil Nadu. *The presentation focused on the efforts in Karnataka.* The establishment of the EWR federation was done as a project of the SSF during 2000 to 2005 with the purpose of federating women elected to local government bodies. Efforts were focused on Collective Strategising (a formal collective identity of women that can enable their voices to be heard) and Value of Network (harmonizing the internal and external transformations of knowledge). The objectives of this exercise were:

- To strengthen local self-government through the collective assertion of political power.
- To transform local governments through greater decentralisation and mainstreaming gender into local governance.
- To bring in, with greater effectiveness the voice, the concerns and the ideas of women into governance through networking with women's groups.
- To enable the associations in creating a collective women's entity and to articulate and negotiate political and economic agendas both at state and national levels.

  Across nine districts of Karnataka, 680 members formed the federation of SSF. While the project phase got over, the Karnataka Federation continued. At the same time, another state level effort of creating a federation of elected women representatives was started—Karnataka Rajaya Chunahiti Mahila Okutta

> *(Karachuma) and the federation members felt that they should merge with this initiative. However, after some time, some EWRs were disillusioned with the Karachuma[9] process and decided to separate and set up Stree Suchana Sangama (SSS) across three districts in North Karnataka—Bijapur, Koppal and Bagalkot. This was registered under the Societies Registration Act in 2006-07 and continues its activities offering permanent membership to EWRs, past and present.*

Structure

Federation efforts in Karnataka were done across 9 districts and enrolled 680 members. While the project phase got over, the Karnataka Federation continued. At the same time, another state level effort of creating a federation of elected women representatives was started—Karnataka Rajaya Chunahiti Mahila Okutta (Karachuma) and the federation members felt that they should merge with this initiative.

However, after some time, some EWRs were disillusioned with the Karachuma process and decided to separate and set-up Stree Suchana Sangama (SSS) across three districts in North Karnataka–Bijapur, Koppal and Bagalkot. This was registered under the Societies Registration Act in 2006-07 and continues its activities offering permanent membership to EWRs, past and present.

At the state level, SSS has 12 members in the Executive. These are elected positions from members chosen at the Taluka level. Around 200 EWRs are currently members of SSS across the three districts. They pay an annual membership of Rs. 100. Stree Suchana Sangama (SSS) has some support from local NGOs.

Activities and Achievements

Activities include capacity building on Panchayati Raj, identification of advocacy issues and enabling women to assert their rights and voices. SSS counts in its achievements:

- a successful PEVAC process,
- demand for 50 per cent reservation for women,
- for a full 5 year term for President/Vice-President[10],

- participating in the Panchayati Raj Hakkodaya Andolan[11] and undertaking local level advocacy. It actively participated in pre-election voter awareness campaign and provided inputs to 170 women candidates out of which 105 got elected. The process of inducting these new members is currently underway.

Challenges and Lessons

- Collective of EWRs after elections is a difficult process and sustained effort is needed to mobilise them. This is made difficult due to the lack of financial resources. The experience has shown that a new beginning has to be made every five years after the elections and these impacts on the sustainability of the federation.
- A critical element is to ensure that the federation has to be strong at the block level to create any effective forum at the state level.

2.7 Sugrama Grama Panchayat Chunayita Mahila Prathinidhigala Sangha Karnataka[12]

Introduction

SUGRAMA is a newly emerging EWR federation in Karnataka. The federation building process is supported by The Hunger Project in partnership with local NGOs across the state. SUGRAMA sought to build upon the experiences of the earlier attempts of creating federations in the state, especially those of EWRs. It was an articulated need that emerged from EWRs after the 2005 elections in the state to have a common platform for a collective voice at the political level and to act as a pressure group to demand for rights and powers from the government.

After 2005-06 elections, The Hunger Project partner organisations conducted trainings for 3,217 EWRs on issues around Federations across 53 blocks of the state. This process was accompanied by developing a White Paper on components of EWR Federations to assess the learnings from previous experiences. The Hunger Project invited SKL International and SIPU from Sweden to technically support this process. An interim steering committee was established with seven EWRs representing eight districts. Working groups were formed to brainstorm role and structure of the federation and an exposure visit to Sweden was organised to understand the role of Swedish local governments in federation process.

Structure

SUGRAMA is registered under the Societies Act with a vision of "empowered elected Gram Panchayat women representatives in a gender just and equal society" and the goal "to empower GP-EWRs to collectively advocate and practice good governance for the overall development of the Gram Panchayats". The Federation has expanded from 53 to 87 talukas across 22 districts. There are currently demands for the expansion to new districts due to the visibility during the PEVAC process.

GOVERNANCE STRUCTURE

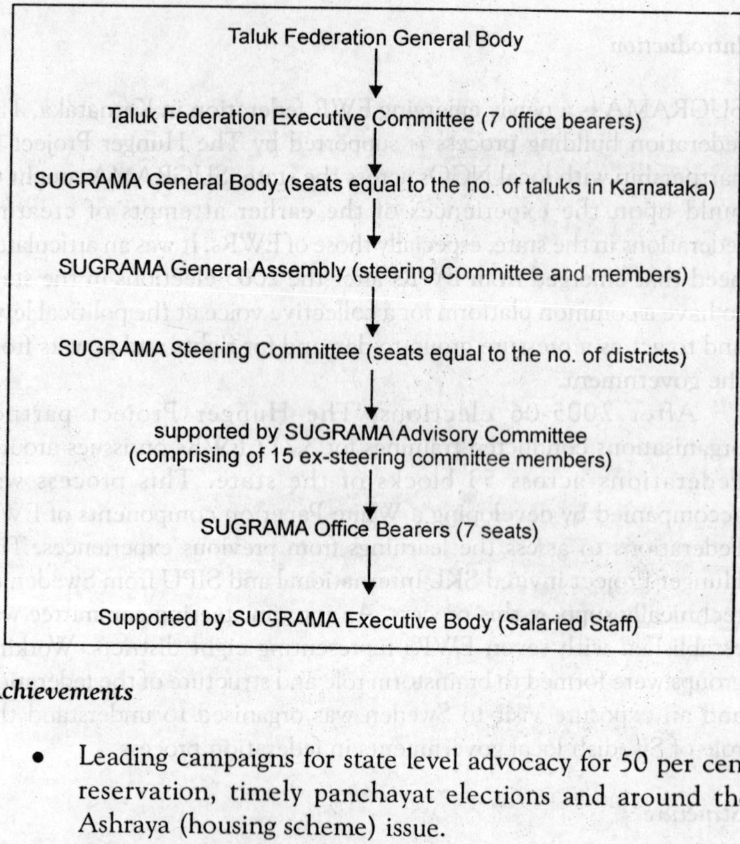

Achievements

- Leading campaigns for state level advocacy for 50 per cent reservation, timely panchayat elections and around the Ashraya (housing scheme) issue.
- Holding a press conference to highlight the challenges faced by panchayat representatives.
- Members sought to ensure that the right people get the allocation for houses under the housing scheme. The Federation has advocated for honorarium for Panchayat members and for financial transparency in Panchayats.
- The Federation has supported members facing violence and has been able to develop a rapport with the government and bureaucracy.

Challenges and Lessons

The Federation seeks to increase membership while also regrouping after the recent elections. They see the taluka unit is vital for the federation and seek to increase the visibility across the state. SUGRAMA already have a paid employee and they want to ensure that sufficient resources are available for the person to continue functioning. Political aspirations of the EWRs may make SUGRAMA shaky in the future and effort is being made to ensure that all members are clear about the goal and objectives of the Federation.

2.8 SUTRA[13] (Social Uplift Through Rural Action): Decentralised Governance: Experience of Working with Women Representatives of Panchayats

Introduction

SUTRA (Social Uplift Through Rural Action) has been working to establish a non-discriminatory governance at all levels—from home to State. The organisation works directly in three blocks of two districts of Himachal Pradesh and in another 20 blocks across 5 districts with partner organisations. Areas of intervention include:

- domestic violence free Panchayats
- autonomous Nyaya (judicial) Panchayats
- decline in girl child sex ratio
- socio-economic exclusion of single women
- gender and health, reproductive rights
- economic empowerment of women
- roofwater harvesting

Activities

Interventions with Panchayats were begun in 1986-87 based on the complaints by Mahila Mandal members that Panchayat members do not listen to them when domestic violence issues are reported. Gender sensitisation interventions were made. SUTRA's interventions over the past years have shown that panchayats can be activated to work on gender issues. That EWR federations can successfully make their voices heard, social justice can be delivered through Panchayats if proper training and orientation is held and that Gram Sabhas are willing to debate and discuss issues of domestic violence and reproductive rights.

Achievements

SUTRA has been able to make significant changes. Some of these being:

- Abolishment of 2 child norm in Himachal Pradesh.
- Organising 7,000 single women to form collectives and fight against discrimination.
- More than 300 GPs regularly conduct Mahila Gram Sabhas, some twice a year.
- EWRs have started federating.
- Panchayats actively work towards arresting declining sex ratio.

Challenges

The Challenges faced by SUTRA are to develop a strategy of engaging Panchayats to work on safeguarding reproductive rights. Engaging with Panchayat to create an enabling environment for participation of Dalit women members, provide decisive EWRs physical safety and social dignity, and creating democratic functioning of Panchayats and reducing the importance of Panchayat Secretary. Given the hilly terrain, making up-Gram Sabha active is important.

While funds to Panchayats have gone up, insufficient investment is being made in enabling them to handle these funds and funds are being spent in the names of Panchayats without the leaders being able to control this. Devolution in itself is not sufficient—democratisation of society is critical. With increasing amounts of funds being spent through the gram panchayats, they have become a terrain for competitive politics reducing space for independent women. Given that Himachal Pradesh is a small state, new entrants to politics face serious challenge from existing politicians.

2.9 Goa Panchayat Mahila Shakti Abhiyan[14]

Introduction

The Grama Panchayat Mahila Shakti Abhiyan was formed in Goa in 2007. Goa being a small state, there are no intermediate panchayats. The Vision and Mission of GPMSA are:

- Facilitate Democratic Decentralisation and Strengthen Local Governance through the grassroots level institutions like Gram Sabhas and Panchayats.
- Empowering elected Panchayat members including Women and Youth to build strong movements in developments and democracy at the grassroots.
- Holistic Development of all sections of the Society through Panchayati Raj governance.
- Participatory Planning and Sustainable Rural Development
- Maximise people's participation to generate optimum utilisation of the resources.
- Support the Co-operative Movement through NGOs, SHGs, Mahila and Yuva Mandals, rural agencies etc. to ensure economic sustainability.
- Provide need based support to all stakeholders to generate maximum efficiency in the day to day capacity mobilisation.

- Promote community development initiatives by sensitisation and awareness through the IEC mode.
- Ensure Good Governance through ICTs to realise the goal of knowledge society in the country through the implementation of Five Year Plans.
- Achieve the successful realisation of MDGs put forth by the United Nations Organisation.

Structure

- The GPMSA has 31 members representing all the EWRs of 189 Gram Panchayats and two Zilla Panchayats. It has a General Body and Governing Body, two district Committees and 11 Block Committees.
- The GPMSA is registered under the Society Registration Act and under the Goa Co-operative Act. Registration process was completed in 2008.
- The managing committee meets once a month. Members are paid a conveyance allowance. Taluka and District Committees were formed through elections among EWRs conducted by the Directorate of Panchayats. These committees then elected the State Committee. Since there was an overlap between the term of the office bearers of the PMSA and those of the Panchayats after the recent elections, an amendment has been made to make the terms in both the Panchayat term and that of Goa-PMSA co-terminus so positions are occupied by serving EWRs.

Activities

The PMSA has been able to tap the Central and state government for funds. 12 lakh Rupees were given by the Central Government while the state government has extended a rent free space to create the State Support Centre. In addition, funds from MPLADS (Members of Parliaments Load Area Development Scheme) were mobilised for office fixtures and furniture. The State government also provides Rs. 5 lakhs annually as well as a vehicle. The GPMSA was actively involved in raising the issue of SEZs in Goa. Series of collaborative

efforts have been made with the Department of Science and Technology, the State Women Commission and the Health Department. Advocacy efforts focus around the devolution of funds, functions and functionaries.

Achievements

GPMSA has been able to raise its profile in a short period. This has been possible through the mobilisation of funds from various departments and carrying out grassroots level activities. The PMSA has served as an effective mechanism for EWRs across the state to interact with each other and to advocate for greater devolution of funds, functions and functionaries to the Panchayats.

Challenges

Goa being a small state, there is a lot of interference from MLAs in local affairs and causes conflicts with panchayat functionaries.

PART 3
ISSUES FLAGGED IN THE WORKSHOP

At the end of the presentations on Day 1, a list of issues to be discussed over the next day was prepared. In the opening remarks, the organising team had proposed that discussion on the federations could be done in three broad themes, having a choice of adding or changing the themes suggested. The themes proposed were:

- Membership/Form/Structure of the Federations Vision/ Mission/Mandate of existing federations and related issues.
- Sustainability/Autonomy/Legitimacy.

LoGIn had already listed some broad themes and issues. During the day, as new issues came up, they were clustered in three broad themes.

Membership/Form/Structure: Internal democracy, role of NGOs v/s Federation, scale and coverage, criteria of membership (fixed /former EWR/SHG members/men), conflict management, engagement with—Dalits/minorities/political parties, integration of members from three-tiers of PRI, approach for federation formation—top down or build from below, form of federation—institution, organisation, formal registration, by-laws, gatekeepers.

Sustainability/Autonomy/Legitimacy: Future perspective, fund raising, strategic growth plan, performance or effectiveness indicators.

Vision/Mission/Mandate

Origin and dynamics leading to formation of federation, evolution

and changes, agenda setting-capacity building/support/helpline/advocacy, nature—Programme/movement/organisation, address larger governance issues, address larger issues of decentralisation, feminist understanding and practice of power, role of Federation during elections, Implications of 50 per cent reservation, inability of women/Dalits to contest from 'general seats'.

PART 4
SYNTHESIS

At the beginning of Day 2, the discussants were invited to share their observations, consolidate the presentation, recapitulate the discussions and raise issues to analyse the experience.

Address by Dr. R. K. Singh

Dr. Singh discussed the wide variation seen in the presentations and recognised that these were due to the variety of context—both in terms of location as well as time. He observed that there does not seem to have been significant cross-learning opportunities, except for the Tamil Nadu, Kerala and Karnataka Federations as they were supported by the same source. A clear message that emerged is that the mandate of the federations was influenced not only by the context but also the position of the facilitating agency.

Typology

He noted that there were variations in the experiences, while some thought registration was not needed, others were comfortable with registration. Nomenclatures such as networks, federation, movement, institution were used and often interchangeably. There appeared a wide variation around issue-based coalition as with membership (where some limited it to Gram Panchayats, some to Presidents, some across PRI tiers, some with former EWRs and others with SHG members and life members). Funding support was also from a diverse mix like MoPR, Membership fees, local resource mobilisation. Various support organisations were mentioned—NGOs, group of NGOs, State Training Institutes, Activists-feminists, SHG, Youth groups etc.

Mandate

Wide variations in mandate were seen but there was a commonality in a focus on issues around social and gender justice. Common policy issues emerging were the demand for 50 per cent reservation, reservations for two terms for all seats, challenging the two-child norm and in some cases specific struggles against regressive schemes like SAMRAS consensus. At the operational issue four visible patterns were taking up corruption, budgets, grievance redressal and pattern of interaction/engagement with family, officials linked with a sense of dignity. Capacity building was taken up across various issues—that of legal literacy, schemes, budgets, leadership development, knowledge sharing, helplines, perspective building on issues related to women and social justice (minorities and dalits), accountability and transparency.

Strategy

The experience of federation building is fairly new with all experiences shared being less than ten years. A clear trend visible is that there is a mix of urgent and long-term issues that the federations are rising.

They are also in a process of expanding their scope and scale. All experience showed that there are not sufficient external resources for such a process and the federations are striving for having the maximum impact with the limited resources. The use of the media to advocate for issues was clearly brought out by the presentations. Wide difference in experience of the engagement of the support agency were also seen—some of the federations emerged from below and the support agency facilitated the process while others were planned/ designed externally and EWRs invited to participate in the process. Positioning of most support groups seem to be of promoting Federations to take a lead around issues.

Outcomes

Federations have claimed changes in policies and have noticed that the collective engagement and visibility has changed the pattern of interaction with government/bureaucracy. Reporting of increased self-confidence and participation in governance emerged from all presentations as was the focus on well-being of women regarding their status and violence etc. Recognition of EWR leaders and that of the federation by political parties were also discussed.

Sustainability

All presentations highlighted the role of the external agency and dependence seems to be very high, the other issue of concern is that there is a high rate of attrition due to the cyclical nature of election. Some of the federations have sought to address this issue through life memberships, membership for former EWRs, etc. Regarding some of the relatively older experiences, he noted that the momentum of the federations slowed down due to the resource crunch—an issue linked with the withdrawal of funding for the support agency. Issues of co-option by political parties as well as leadership were discussed while keeping socio-political environment in mind.

> *The participants were urged to undertake a dispassionate analysis of experiences and refine the typology observed. Advantages and disadvantages of each approach need to be critically examined*

and the assumptions need to be clearly articulated. This was thought of as being helpful in devising a way forward.

Address by Ms. Alyamma Vijayan

Ms. Vijayan took forward the points raised by Dr. Singh. The visible diversity in the experience were due to the fact that different states are at a different developmental stage, devolution is at different levels and that determines the nature of capacity building initiatives that need to be undertaken. Other relevant issues are the levels of education among the people as well as electoral candidates, the level of politicisation of the society as well as the status of women. This does not allow an easy comparison of experiences and typology will necessarily differ for each experience. Women have not experienced formal power and were new to power after being elected to Panchayat positions without much experience/resources. Being part of a collective helps them in overcoming the hesitation and gives them the power of solidarity.

The terms Federation/Network/Forum were used interchangeably and emphasised that each word has an underlying meaning denoting the density of engagement. The objective of the collective may determine its structure.

Long-term goals did not come through clearly—as a collective one should be able to make substantive changes in governance. There has to be clarity in the purpose—if the collective focuses on better implementation of programmes or getting more power. The group was asked to reflect if the Women Collectives are addressing new types of leadership, of having a position on broader issues and having a perspective linking local to global issues—for example GM seeds.

Capacity building was interpreted and understood differently by people. There is a need for proper perspective building. Former EWRs and core group of trainers can play a vital role to make federations more effective. Needs assessment of the requirement of members is critical. There has to be clarity in collectives on the position about women who are interested in broader politics, as also on their accountability. The Mahila Samakya example in the 1990s showed how EWRs would use the Sangha for feedback but would also be accountable to them. A critical element is whether federations are able to create democratic practices within their structure and decision-making.

The role of support organisations becomes critical when they engage with women in politics as a number of them want to stay away from mainstream political processes while the EWR members cannot or may not want to do the same. Overall, it is important for the members of the federation to have a sense of ownership over it.

Women collectives have the potential to transform politics and that women leadership from these bodies being co-opted by political parties is a positive sign and should be seen as an indicator of success. However, with increasing party control over the emerging women politicians, the maneuvering space may reduce for such collectives. The five year term is a challenge for long-term sustainability for such collectives and they need to creatively plan out to enable continuity.

Address by Dr. Joy Elamon

As the final discussant, Dr. Elamon noted that most of the Federations are managed/supported by NGOs. He posed whether EWR Federations sought to use Panchayati Raj for women's empowerment or worked on women empowerment to strengthen Panchayati Raj Institutions, or engaged with women empowerment to deepen democracy. There are state-wise variations in the experiences shared. Sometimes resources can actually become a problem if federation get used to operating with sufficient resources and cannot sustain the process once funds dry up. Some continuity in leadership as well as membership is needed for transfer of knowledge as new members come into the Federation.

NGOs supporting EWR federations should have clear norms regarding boundaries. There has been a lot of discussion around co-option of the Federation by the State/ Political parties but co-option by NGOs was not discussed. EWR Federations are essentially political, but their engagement shouldn't just be seen to be with political parties. However, once EWR start challenging/questioning supporting NGOs, it shows that the collective is becoming autonomous.

While registration may lead to formal recognition–it may also lead to diminished power. It is best to seek recognition through action. The Federation should support the EWRs to take up broader issues around development and social justice rather than just taking up women issues. A number of networks exist in the same location—being of different scales—national, state or local level. This can either strengthen or weaken the process and is a challenge. There exist a number of associations at the local level but most people do not know about them. Similarly, All India Panchayat Associations exist but are not very visible.

After inputs from the discussants, there was a quick recap on the themes and issues that had been flagged the previous day we arranged into the three themes. Three groups were made, with each group to discuss all the three themes. Moderators for each group were decided and three people in each group were requested to act as rapporteurs for each of the themes respectively. After the group discussions, the rapporteurs for each theme across the three groups collectively consolidated the discussion per theme. The consolidated presentation from the rapporteurs capturing the discussions from each group is reported below. Each presentation was followed by further discussion on the theme.

PART 5
THEMATIC DISCUSSION

Theme 1: Vision/Mission/Mandate

The discussion looked at the process as well as elements. The group was clear that it should be the prerogative of the EWRs to define the vision, mission and mandate for any federation. This should be done through the identification of the views of the EWRs and women, both at a general level as well as those specific to the area.

- Focussing on the elements, these should have a broad framework covering issues of social justice while highlighting issues specific to the area.
- They should be pragmatic, realistic and reasonable. It should be according to the socio-cultural environment and should address both immediate and long-term aspiration.
- The Vision should be broad and not just focus on women, highlight social justice issues without losing focus on issues important to women and women leaders.
- The Mission should address rights, address hindrance of the system, highlight advocacy role with the state and transforming the PDC.
- The Mandate should be to nurture leadership, capacity building, helpline support cell, information collection.
- Federations need to look at:
  - ➢ Negotiating with political parties: The Federations having a political identity, they need to work externally in defining their relationship with political parties.
  - ➢ Political Education (undertake party and reformative politics): Education of the members around political parties as well as arriving at political positions through an informed debate and discussion are critical for any Federation to retain in vibrancy.
- Additionally, as safeguards Federations need to ensure that there is:
  - ➢ Emphasis on constitutional values.
  - ➢ Achievements are not at the expense of systems, procedures and structures.
  - ➢ A clear set of non-negotiable are collectively understood and defined.
- Retaining flexibility is a challenge for the support organisation as their perspectives and beliefs sometimes define the Federation in its own image. This leads to the federations not being flexible enough to respond to changing circumstances. Similarly, experience has shown that there is divergence between the precept and practice as far as our Constitution is concerned. A clear strategy to bridge this is needed as EWRs can also see that political parties that do

not adhere to the Constitution can work effectively on the ground.

- The mandate for an advocacy role for Federation was debated in the plenary with a broad acceptance that it is a necessary role. While some opinions saw this as the main focus for federations, other saw this part of the role in giving the Federation recognition and mainstreaming it in the political discourse. In certain cases, it is also important to choose advocacy issues strategically for any emerging federation as any lack of success over a period of time may adversely impact the Federation itself.
- The mandate should emphasise the focus on Women. While Panchayat Unions can take up issues related to decentralisation, the emphasis should be around issues related to women. Confidence and expansion of knowledge has shown new leadership focussing on women issues and fighting patriarchal values.

Theme 2: Membership/Form/Structure

The consolidated presentation sought to create an ideal structure based on the discussion among the three groups.

- The basic unit should be at the block level with a State level core group. At the Gram Panchayat/village level, there should be members from EWRs, former EWRs and potential women candidates. However, after that, the federation should only have EWR representation at the Block, District, Region (group of around 3 districts) and State level. The Structure should be flexible and determined according to the needs of the Federation.
- Membership should be open for all EWRs across the three PRI tiers and women leaders. The Federation should have formal membership and enrolment should be done through a membership form. The membership fees should be decided by the Federation. The membership term may be permanent and based on periodic renewal. While acknowledging the need for the Federation to have EWRs across the three tiers

of the PRIs, the team cautioned that inter-level rivalries would have to be controlled as Block and District level members can use the Federation and/or the support organisation for their own power.

Discussions around this theme raised the following issues:

- *Federation should be level or area based:* Experiences from the previous day threw up both kinds of examples with Associations of GP Presidents, those of GP members as also those across the three-tiers. The local context would ultimately decide this.
- *District as ideal unit:* It become difficult to manage regular interactions beyond a district level and while the basic units are formed at block level, district seems an ideal level for the Federations as significant opportunities for negotiation exist at this level. A loose coalition of Federations at the state level rather than having a structure heavy state level federation may be more useful. Issue based consolidation of efforts may prove to be better advocacy vehicles.
- *Level of Federation/network of federations*: To be able to address policy issues and advocate its interests, Federations have to link up with each other at the state and even the national level. This does not mean that a national level federation is necessarily needed, and may not be needed at all, but there is a clear need for a platform that permits that exchange of views, consolidation and its articulation as policy speak. With the Central Government making a number of policies, some by passing the states government and Panchayati Raj Institutions, engagement at the national level for Federations is becoming crucial. Apart from such engagement, federations have been and should engage with broader platforms and issues.
- *Basis of membership*: Experiences from earlier showed a broad mix, of EWRs, SHGs members, potential leaders, past leaders etc. Federations help women have a additional sense of identity through which they derive strength. A clear formulation of the role of the all constituents, the benefits

that they can draw and the strength that they bring in should be articulated and this should form the basis of membership to the Federations. Clearly identified barriers to entry and exit from membership are needed. Members should feel obligated to work towards the goals of the Federation.

- *Formal registration or not—its advantages/weaknesses*: While registration creates rigidity, a formal identity is needed when the Federation engages with the state or while scaling it up. Thus, registration needs to be strategic because it is not needed at the action level.

Theme 3: Sustainability (Legitimacy/Autonomy)

The consolidated presentation highlighted the following:

- *Legitimacy*: Registration is seen as important to have legitimacy with the state. This in turn is decided by the objectives of the Federation. As a federation scales up and increases coverage, it loses its informal arrangements and personal knowledge and rapport, a formal identity is helpful. Linkages with government programmes can be helpful in seeking legitimacy from the government. This can even be in the form of working with the Panchayat Mahila Shakti Abhiyan. A review of the guidelines of the PMSA and policy advocacy for them to be more flexible should be taken up.
- Support organisations should have a clear exit policy and a well understood and realistic support and exit plan and mechanism with the Federation to enable it to effectively undertake management as the support organisations withdraws with time.
- Regular membership drives and seeking sponsorship are important for the federation to grow and be visible and raise its own resources.
- Continuous engagement of present and past members.
- Different model of financial sustainability need to be understood for Federations to have financial and managerial autonomy. It is also critical to do a resource mapping of domestic sources of funds, including from the government as well as CSR arms of industry to support such initiatives.

- Among others, the quality of leadership development and capacity building in the federation determines its ability to have a legitimate and autonomous position.
- There was a detailed discussion amongst the participants on the merits of registering the Federation. Moreover, an opinion put to the floor was that the Federation can remain unregistered, but the Technical Support Unit that provides support to the Federation may be registered and can, besides doing its primary function, undertake fund raising. Dependency on NGOs can only be broken as the Technical Support Unit takes over most of the support functions over time.

PART 6
CONSOLIDATION AND FOLLOW-UP

The final day of the workshop included an interaction with the Dr. Hrushikesh Panda, Additional Secretary, Ministry of Panchayati Raj and a presentation on ALGI and the lessons drawn during the workshop. Also a brief input was given by Mr. T. R. Raghunandan, consultant to LoGIn, on professional services that local governments need and use of technology for learning and upscaling good practices.

From the Ministry of Panchayati Raj

Dr. Panda shared with the group that currently the MoPR is developing guidelines to a national level panchayat network. He clarified that this would not mean creating a parallel body of associations but will build representation from below with the GP elected one member to the IP. At the IP level, the committee will be formed of elected members from each tier. At the district level, one ward member, one Sarpanch, one intermediary Panchayat member, intermediary Panchayat President, district Panchayat member and district Panchayat President will form the executive committee.

They will then choose members for the national panchayat. The number of members from the states will not be equal but that there are 4 categories based on population size of the states. The election process should be part of the panchayat process and there are no plans for undertaking this as a separate exercise. While the state Secretariats may be located at the respective SIRDs, that is the decision to be made by state governments. There is no provision for reservation in this and that the PMSA will continue in its present form.

The broad feedback from the group was that:

1. The MOPR should consider getting feedback on the guidelines before implementing them.
2. It may be useful to do a consultation with existing federations to sharpen the conceptual understanding and may be even have a advisory group to guide the process.
3. The entire structure seems too complicated and would be cumbersome to manage.
4. With no reservation, the present structure will end up excluding the voices of the women, especially from the SC/ST and minorities.

Association of Local Governance of India (ALGI)[15]

LGI was formed in 2006 after a preparatory phase of three years, including 4 regional conventions and 11 workshops of elected women representatives. The Objectives of ALGI are to:

- Act as an advocacy and influence group promoting the interests of local government and the decentralisation process in India.
- Network with other associations and individuals who are concerned with the devolution of functions and powers to local government institutions.
- Undertake research and provide specialised services to the members of the Society on matters related to local governments in obtaining their Constitutional and legal entitlements.

- Invite experts from the field of public administration, local governance, development planning, socio-economic studies to provide inputs to the association.

ALGI is a registered society with individual and institutional members. Membership is open to all those interested in promoting local governance. Current members span 20 states across the country. Its secretariat is currently located at Institute of Social Sciences, New Delhi. A National Council meets bi-annually to review progress and plan ahead while the Governing Body decides on policy issues. It is a new initiative and is taking time to establish its credibility within the development sector. Operating on a small team, the outreach has been limited so far. Experience over the past few years has shown that it is easier to work with civil society groups than with PRI functionaries directly and ALGI is now seeking to work with NGOs that work with panchayat leaders.

Lessons Emerging from the Workshop

After the two presentations of the day, participants were requested to reflect on the learnings that they had derived that they would want to pass on to other federations are relevant issues to keep in mind. These could relate to principles, operational suggestions and/or positions. These were written on cards and consolidated. A listing of helpful tips, not all of which are mutually reinforcing, emerged out of this process.

Some Principles Emerging from the Workshop

- A focus on need based activities brought results and sustainability to federations.
- If the potential is tapped, federations can expand and achieve much more.
- Connectedness raises hopes and confidence among EWRs.
- Process oriented federations add values and strengthen the structure.
- Mutual learning and experience sharing builds solidarity among EWRs.
- Main resource is the collective itself, with availability of funds or external recognition playing a minor part.
- Federations can become a classroom for learning and practice of democratic values and transparency.
- Relevance of a federation is subject to what extent it has succeeded in providing solutions to problems of PRIs, Elected representatives, or people at large.

Some Prescriptions for Federations

Vision/Mission/Mandate

- Goal should be a discrimination free society.
- Focus on political understanding of class, caste, gender, politics.
- Federations should evolve through a consultative process.
- Issues to be addressed should be identified by the federation.
- Prepare the ground first, before launching a Federation building process.
- Federation should not emerge as a parallel body.
- Advocacy is a critical role that Federation should play.
- Federations need to address policy level issues.

Membership/Form/Structure

- Issues of membership and structure to be deliberated regularly.
- Federation units should have periodic meetings.
- Leadership focus is essential to strengthen leadership within federations.
- Representation of the marginalised should be ensured.
- Form sub-federations (dalits, minorities, transgender).
- Should be facilitated by NGOs.
- Should be a ward member federation.
- Work at GP, Block and ZP level.
- The basic unit of the Federation should be at the block level.
- Coordination across federations in a state.

Sustainability

- Need for self-sufficiency of funds is critical and resource mobilisation plans should be developed.

Support Organisations

- Build a platform to strengthen linkage between NGOs.
- Membership growth of ALGI.
- Cooperation between Federations and SIRDs (organic relationships).
- A loose coalition at state level of organisations supporting Panchayati Raj Institutions should also extend support to EWR federations.

Questions to be asked while Forming Federations

- Is there a preparedness to be organised?
- What should be the approach: top down or bottom up?
- What is the issue of sustainability when the federation is donor driven?

Others

- Federations require long-term broad base support as it takes time to get established and raise its own resources.

Needs and Opportunities Emerging from the Workshop

Detailed discussions around each of the points emerging out of the lessons took place. After the discussion, the moderator steered the discussion to emerging needs and opportunities arising out of this workshop. LoGIn could provide a platform if there was interest in taking some identified issues forward. While a number of people made their inputs, Raghunandan made a presentation on the services that his upcoming organisation wants to provide to the Panchayati Raj Institutions and which may be of interest to Federations as well. He shared the services provided by his Company including circular information service, fund release information service, mapping, weekly commentaries of government Policies related to decentralisation, helpline, mapping as well as specific demand driven services. His thrust was that these services can now be provided at a very low cost in a timely manner through the use of ICT technology. He also shared the example of horizontal learning programmes in the Union Parishads in Bangladesh and how effective cross learning between Union Parishad members has been taking place. Opportunities were shared by participants and these were consolidated after an open discussion. A listing of emerging needs was generated through this process, these being:

Knowledge/Documentation

- Descriptive Analysis that describes the goals, processes, interventions of the federation will help others to draw lessons.
- Create Usable Knowledge that can be used to inform other Federations.
- Evidence Based Research which challenges assertions and options are needed to understand this emerging phenomenon.
- Publications that address different stakeholders should be developed.

Information Needs

- A collection of material targeted at elected representatives needs to be collected and shared.

- National and State Directories on Existing Federations would help in knowing the role and scope of the existing federations.
- Contacts/Address of all federations and contact of ALGI – Establishing Linkages.
- Sharing of State Government Orders/Resolutions with EWR federation to keep them informed is important.
- Incorporate Technology to scale-up for information dissemination, real time feedback and capacity building as the size of Federations increase.
- Tie-up with retired Bureaucrats who can guide the Federations on understanding Government Orders as well as negotiating the bureaucracy.

Values and Perspectives

- Federations should emphasize, build and strengthen political perspective amongst members.
- Perspective building of the members on role of Power and Domination should be a primary role of the Federation.
- Value based politics needs to be promoted. This allows women associated with different political parties to come together in the same federation.

Strengthening a Federation

- Building federations requires a process of capacity development and preparing the EWRs, the concept of a collective either grows organically or needs to be introduced once the initial engagement occurs.
- Process design is critical to setting up a EWR federation.
- New ideas for federation building should be evaluated as this is still a learning process.
- Indicators for process and outcomes need to be developed to assess the state of EWR federations.
- Exposure visit of EWRs to different federations will expose them to other perspectives.
- Platform for Policy Advocacy is needed at the state and central levels and this should engage effectively with EWR federations.

Role of Support Organisation

- Values of the support organisation with minorities—while Representation of the SC/ST/OBCs is assured through reservation, those of minorities is still low. The support organisations need to recognise this and integrate this into their interventions.
- The support organisations should be facilitative and not impose their own ideology/perspective on the Federation and be in a position to give informed choices to the members of the Federation.
- Role Clarity on Support Organisation is critical. This requires further discussion and elaboration.
- Capacity building of NGOs is important as a number of cases have highlighted the fact that there is a number of NGOs across the state providing support to Federations.

Conclusion and Follow-up

While the discussion established the need for information and knowledge requirements, it needs to be clearly defined what exactly the federations require. Moreover, an emerging issue is to develop clear monitoring indicators in relation to the process of federation building so that expansion, deepening and intensive growth can be assessed. The discussions also threw up issues regarding the agency of the EWRs with respect both to the Federation as well as the Support Organisation. The critical role that support organisations play in the success of a Federating process needs to be further explored. Upward political mobility of EWRs at the Gram Panchayat level was an interesting learning that came up in these discussions. The role of Collectives/Federations in this should be further explored. Another point of discussion was the creative tension between these collectives functioning as an organisation versus as a movement and how they related to the broader social change movements around them. Availability of disembodied technological resources to facilitate easy communication is another opportunity toward capacity building and information exchange.

NOTES AND REFERENCES

1. A guideline for the presentations had been shared with the participants with a request to cover the listed points. This is attached as Appendix 2.
2. List of participants attached in Appendix 3.
3. The Presentation on the MRA was jointly made by Nandatai Gaekwad, Sarpanch from Maharashtra and Bhim Raskar, Director, RSCD.
4. Presentation made by Dr. Palanithurai, Professor, Gandhigram Rural University.
5. Presentation made jointly by Avani Rawal from MSA, Hansaben Gamar, Sarpanch from Gujarat, and Lata Sachde from KMVS.
6. Presentation made by C.V. Shyamala from CWS and G. Aruna, Vice President of the AP EWR Association.
7. Presentation made by Ashwini Palewal from Astha Sansthan and Pushpa Shreemali, former Sarpanch.
8. Presentation made by Mangala Gudimath and Soman Kolar from SSF. SUGRAMA presentation was also made after this and questions and clarifications were made after both presentations.
9. The Karachuma initiative has now become ineffectual.
10. The Karnataka Panchayati Raj Act stipulates elections to the post of President and Vice-President of the Panchayat after two and a half years of the term through the elected members of the Panchayats.
11. A state level network of stakeholders working for effective functioning of Panchayati Raj Institutions in Karnataka.
    The link shows a list of members- http://www.workingchild.org/0607/htm%2006%2007/The%20Constitutional%20Rights%20of%205653%20Grama20Panchayats%20of%20Karnataka.htm, including a large number of Panchayat Federations operational in the state.
12. Presentation made by Reshma from THP Bangalore and M. Renuka Rama Reddy, President, SUGRAMA.
13. Presentation made by Subhash Mendhapurkar from SUTRA.
14. Presentation made by Nelly J. Rodrigues, Zila Panchayat Member, South Goa.
15. Presentation made by Ms. Nelly Rodriguez, member ALGI Executive Committee.

APPENDIX-1

Schedule of Workshop

Day 1 – 7th September, 2010

Time	Agenda
10.00 onwards	Tea and Snacks at the Conference Hall (Ball room)
11.00-11.30	Opening Remarks: Rational for the workshop and; introduction of all the participants.
11.30-11.45	Design of the workshop and expected outputs
11.45-12.00	***Tea/Coffee Break***
12.00-12.30	1st Presentation: RSCD and Mahila Rajsatta Andolan, Maharashtra
12.30-13.00	2nd Presentation: Gandhigram, Tamil Nadu
13.00-14.00	***Lunch Break***
14.00-14.30	3rd Presentation: Mahila Swaraj Abhiyan and Kutch Mahila Vikas Sangathan, Gujarat
14.30-15.00	4th Presentation: Centre for World Solidarity, Andhra Pradesh
15.00-15.30	***Tea/Coffee Break***
15.30-16.00	5th Presentation: Astha and Mahila Panch Sarpanch Sangthan, Rajasthan
16.00-16.30	6th Presentation: SSM, Karnataka
16.30-17.00	7th Presentation: THP and SUGRAMA, Karnataka
17.00-17.30	8th Presentation: SUTRA, Himachal Pradesh
17.30-17.45	***Break***
17.45-18.15	Consolidation and Flagging issues (by the Discussants)
18.15-18.30	Preparing for the next day (group formation)

Group work for next day: The participants will be divided into *three groups*. Each group will get a chance to discuss on *three thematic areas*. Each group will have *leader per thematic area*. Once all the three discussions have completed in each group, the thematic heads will sit together and work on thematic presentations.

Day 2 – 8th September, 2010

09.00-09.30	Recap and Setting the tone
09.30-10.30	Group discussion on: Membership/Form/Structure
10.30-11.30	Group discussion on: Vision/Mission/Mandate
11.30-11.45	***Tea/Coffee Break***
11.45-12.40	Group discussion on: Sustainability (Legitimacy, Autonomy and Resource sufficiency)
12.45-14.15	***Lunch Break and*** Preparation for the presentation by the Thematic leaders
14.15-15.00	Presentation: Membership/Form/Structure followed by discussion
15.00-15.45	Presentation: Vision/Mission/Mandate followed by discussion
15.45-16.30	Presentation: Sustainability followed by discussion
16.30-17.00	***Tea/Coffee Break***
17.00-17.30	Address by the discussants
17.30-17.45	Wrap up and groups for next day

Day 3 – 9th September, 2010

09.00-09.30	Presentation by ALGI
09.30-10.00	Presentation by MoPR
10.00-11.00	Groups for discussion on Emerging needs and opportunities
11.00-11.30	***Tea/Coffee Break***
11.30-12.15	Presentations
12.15-12.45	Address by the discussants
12.45-13.30	Conclusion and Closure
13.30-14.30	***Lunch***

APPENDIX-2

Structure of Presentations

Scheme of the Presentation to be made by the invited Presenters (10 slides, 20 minutes)

- Overall Context and Rationale/Justification (1 slide)
- Objectives/Mission and Time Line since its inception (1 slide)
- Present status: legal status, organisational structure, coverage area, size, membership, budget, support and resources available (maximum 3 slides)
- Current Activities/Priorities (1 slide) Key Achievements (1 slide) Challenges faced (1 slide)
- Lessons learnt (1 slide)
- Looking Ahead: Short-term and long-term (1 slide)

APPENDIX-3

List of Participants

Sl. No.	Name	Designation/ Organization	Contact Address	Contact Numbers and email id
1.	Bhim Raskar	Director (Programme), RSCD, Maharashtra	C/o Resource and Support Centre for Development (RSCD) RH – IV, C-4, Lane 8, Sector 9 C.B.D. Belapur, Navi Mumbai-400614 Maharashtra	Tel: 022 27577587, 022 27570405, Mob: 9869259194 email : mahila_rajsatta@yahoo.com
2.	Nandatai Gaikwad	Sarpanch, Mahila Rajsatta Andolan	C/o Resource and Support Centre for Development (RSCD) RH – IV, C-4, Lane 8, Sector 9 C.B.D. Belapur, Navi Mumbai-400 614	Tel : 024 51 255147, Mob: 9860095206 email id : mahila_rajsatta@yahoo.com
3.	Lata Sachde	Katch Mahila Vikas Sanghathan, Gujarat	16, Yogeshwar, Ghanshyam Nagar, Bhuj-370001, Gujarat	Tel :02832 223340, 02832 222124 Mob :9426921526 Email : lsachde@yahoo.co.in
4.	Avani Rawal	Network Co-ordinator, Mahila Swaraj Abhiyan, Gujarat	22, Heenapark Society, Nr. Shyamal Row House Part - 5, Kenyug Cross Roads, Satellite, Ahmedabad-380015, Gujarat	Tel :079 26610447, 079 26610447 Mob : 09924936064 email : mahilaswarajabhiyan@gmail.com
5.	Peresis Ginwalla	Independent Consultant, EC Member, Mahila Swaraj Abhiyan, Gujarat	Ginwalla`s Bunglows, Opp. Hotel Le Meridien, Khanpur Road, Ahmedabad-380 001, Gujarat	9825045495 email : persis_ginwalla@yahoo.co.in
6.	Hansaben Gamar	Hingatiya Jagir Gram Panchayat (MSA, Gujarat)	Sarpanch Hingatiya Jagir Gram Panchayat, Khedbrahma Block, Sabarkantha District, Gujarat	Mob :9998954813 email : mahilaswarajabhiyan@gmail.com

(*Contd.*)

Appendix-3 (*Contd.*)

Sl. No.	Name	Designation/ Organization	Contact Address	Contact Numbers & email id
7.	Leela Devi	Sutra, H.P	SUTRA, Ramshahar Village & Post: Ramshahar, District Solan-174 102 Himachal Pradesh	Tel : 01795 258515 email : sutrahp@yahoo.co.in
8.	Subhash Mendhapukar	Director, SUTRA, H.P	SUTRA, Ramshahar Village & Post: Ramshahar, District Solan-174 103 Himachal Pradesh	Tel :01792 283725, 01792 283772, Mob :9418022118 email : sutrahp@yahoo.co.in
9.	Reshma	Programme Associate, The Hunger Project	No. 316/E, 9th Amoir, 40th Cross, 5th Block Jayanagar, Banglore-560041, Karnataka	080 22459115, 9480331638 reshma@thp.org
10.	M. Renuka Rama Reddy	President, SUGRAMA, Karnataka	Gundlahalli, Namagendlu - PO, Gowribidhanur (T), Chikkaballapur (D) 561206, Karnataka	Tel : 08155 214106 Mob :997226139
11.	Suman Kolar	State Executive Member, Stree Suchana Sangam, Karnataka	Mantoor Building, Shastri Nagar, Atni Road, At-post: Tikota Tal & Dist: Bijapur, Karnataka	Mob : 9448752499 email : sumankolhar@gmail.com
12.	Mangala Gudimath	Office bearer, Stree Suchana Sangam (Federation)	Near Vishweshwar Temple Member Aalamel Gram Panchayat Tal: Sindagi, Dist: Bijapur Karnataka	Mob : 9880721981
13.	C.V. Shyamala	Jt. Director, Centre for World Solidarity, A.P	12-13-438, Street No. 1, Tarnaka, Secunderabad 500017, Andhra Pradesh	Tel : 040 27018257, Mob : 9849330649 email : shyamala@cwsy.org
14.	G Aruna	MPP Panchayat Women's Association, A.P.	Polkampally - Village MPP, Addakula-Mandal Mahbubnagar District 509002 Andhra Pradesh	Tel : 0854 5223832 Mob : 9490501033, 9440064914
15.	Ashwini Kr. Paliwal	Astha Sansthan	39, Kharol Colony, Udaipur - 3131 004, Rajasthan	Tel :0294 2451348, 0294 2451391 email : astha39@sancharnet.in

(*Contd.*)

Appendix-3 (*Contd.*)

Sl. No.	Name	Designation/ Organization	Contact Address	Contact Numbers & email id
16.	Pushpa Shreemali	Sanyojika, Mahila Panch Sarpanch Sangathan Khamnor	C/o Astha Sansthan |39, Kharol Colony, Udaipur-3131 004, Rajasthan	Tel : 294 2440024 Mob : 9784162429 email : ewrfedre@gmail.com
17.	G. Palanithurai	Professor, Gandhigram Rural University	Rajiv Gandhi Chair for Panchayati Raj Studies, Dept. of Pol. Sci. & Devt. Admn. Gandhigram Rural Institute - Deemed University Gandhigram-624 302, Dindigul District, Tamil Nadu	Tel : 0451 2451775, 0451 2451063 Mob : 9443189409 email : gpgri_rgc@yahoo.com, gpgri_hung1@rediffmail.com
18.	Aleyamma Vijayan	Independant Consultant, Sakhi-Resource Center for Women	Convent Road, Trivandrum-695035, Kerala	Tel : 0471 2462251 email : sakhi@asianetindia.com
19.	R.K Singh	Director, SIRD, Chattisgarh	Chhattisgarh State Institute of Rural Development Nimora, Raipur-492015, Chhattisgarh	Tel : 0771 2473215 Mob : 09424410069 email:dir.cird@nic.inchh041@ifs.nic.in
20.	Rimpa Verma	Technical Support Officer, SIRD, Chhattisgarh	State Institute of Rural Development Chhattisgarh, Nimora, Raipur-492015, Chhattisgarh	Tel : 771 2473215 Mob : 9425508620 email : rimpa.verma@undp.org
21.	Namita Mishra	Independent Consultant	9/1, Saket Colony, Katul Board, Durg, Chhatisgarh	Tel : 0788 2292748 Mob : 9425508620 email: namitadurg@gmail.com
22.	Nelly J. Rodrigues	Zila Panchayat Member, South Goa	H. No. 100, Godhino Ward, South Goa Zilla Panchayat Calata-Majorda, Salcete-403713, Goa	Tel : 0832 2790317, 0832 2726833, Mob : 9822486765 email : goapmsa@gmail.com
23.	Hrusihkesh Panda	Additional Secretary, Ministry of Panchayati Raj	MoPR, GOI, 6th Floor, Hotel Samrat, Chanakya Puri, New Delhi-110021	Tel : 011 23747911 email : hrusikesh.p@nic.in
24.	Joy Elamon	Moderator, Decentralization Community, UNDP Solutions Exchange	55 Lodhi Estate New Delhi-110 003	Tel : 011 46532333 email : joy.elamon@un.org.in

(*Contd.*)

Appendix-3 (*Contd.*)

Sl. No.	Name	Designation/ Organization	Contact Address	Contact Numbers & email id
25.	T.R.Ragunanthan	Independent Consultant	1 KPTCL Quarters, Hosakerehalli Main Road, Bangalooru-560 085, Karnataka	Mob : 9845749988 email : trraghu@yahoo.com
26.	Adil Ali	Independent Consultant	11 Zakir Bagh, Tower 1 New Delhi-110 025	Mob : 9810946314 email : contact.adila@gmail.com
27.	Preeta Lall	Senior Thematic Advisor, Swiss Agency for Development and Cooperation	Swiss Agency for Development and Cooperation, Chandragupta Marg, Chankyapuri, New Delhi-110 020	Tel : 011 26787819 email : preeta.lall@sdc.net
28.	Sonya Elmer Dettelbacher	Programme Officer, Swiss Agency for Development and Cooperation	Swiss Agency for Development and Cooperation, Chandragupta Marg, Chankyapuri, New Delhi-110 021	Tel : 011 26787819 email : sonya.elmer@sdc.net
29.	Swati Dogra	Programme Officer, LoGIn, Swiss Agency for Development and Cooperation	Swiss Agency for Development and Cooperation, Chandragupta Marg, Chankyapuri, New Delhi-110 022	Tel : 011 26787819 email: swati.dogra@sdc.net

Index